LIMERICK DIOCESAN SYNOD 2016

LIMERICK
DIOCESAN SYNOD 2016

※

A Camino of Hope in the Spirit of Truth

Edited by
KAREN KIELY AND ÉAMONN FITZGIBBON

VERITAS

Published 2022 by
Veritas Publications
7–8 Lower Abbey Street
Dublin 1, Ireland

publications@veritas.ie
www.veritas.ie

ISBN 978-1-84730-988-4

Copyright © Karen Kiely and Éamonn Fitzgibbon, 2022

10 9 8 7 6 5 4 3 2 1

The material in this publication is protected by copyright law. Except as may be permitted by law, no part of the material may be reproduced (including by storage in a retrieval system) or transmitted in any form or by any means, adapted, rented or lent without the written permission of the copyright owners. Applications for permissions should be addressed to the publisher.

A catalogue record for this book is available from the British Library.

Designed by Lir Mac Cárthaigh, Veritas Publications
Printed in Ireland by SPRINT-print Ltd, Dublin

Veritas books are printed on paper made from the wood pulp of managed forests. For every tree felled, at least one tree is planted, thereby renewing natural resources.

Contents

List of Figures 8

Introduction 9
Karen Kiely and Éamonn Fitzgibbon

— PART ONE: SETTING OUT —

CHAPTER ONE: Together on the Way: Pope Francis and
　　Synodality 13
Éamonn Fitzgibbon

CHAPTER TWO: Convoking a Synod 21
Bishop Brendan Leahy

CHAPTER THREE: Journeying Towards the Synod 25
Éamonn Fitzgibbon

CHAPTER FOUR: Preparing the Way: The Preparatory
　　Commission 31
Shane Ambrose

— PART TWO: ON THE WAY —

CHAPTER FIVE: Listening: A Process Involving Many 37
Rosemary O'Connor

Chapter Six: Discerning: Learning a New Art Together....49
Jessie Rogers

Chapter Seven: The Synod in Canon Law............................53
Gerard Garrett

Chapter Eight: Prayer on the Synod Journey..................... 57
Betty Baker and Margaret O'Sullivan

Chapter Nine: Reflections along the Way: 'We Are where we Need to Be'... 63
Éamonn Fitzgibbon

Chapter Ten: Catechesis and the Synod 67
Lorraine Buckley

Chapter Eleven: Communicating the Synod......................71
Noirín Lynch

Chapter Twelve: Facilitating the Synod Process...............77
Martin Kennedy

Chapter Thirteen: Accompanying and Administering the Synod.. 85
Karen Kiely

Chapter Fourteen: Back to the Future: Synod 2016........89
David Bracken

— PART THREE: DESTINATION —

CHAPTER FIFTEEN: The Synod Event 95
Karen Kiely

CHAPTER SIXTEEN: Synod Moments of Grace Sustaining
    Us on a Journey 99
Éamonn Fitzgibbon

CHAPTER SEVENTEEN: Synod Puts Building Blocks in
    Place for the Future: A Priest's Perspective 101
Tony Mullins

CHAPTER EIGHTEEN: The Votes: Interpreting the Data 105
Rosemary O'Connor

CHAPTER NINETEEN: Post-Synod: Was it Worth it? 113
Bishop Brendan Leahy

CONCLUSION 117
Éamonn Fitzgibbon

POSTSCRIPT: What Does a Synodal Process Look Like?
    Pope Francis' Letter on Synodality to the Church in
    Germany 119
Bishop Brendan Leahy

Synodality in the Life and Mission of the Church: Extracts
    from a 2018 International Theological Commission
    Document 125

List of Contributors 131

List of Figures

Figure 5.1: Timeline of the Four Phases 38
Figure 5.2: Eight Models for Listening and Discernment 38
Figure 5.3: Data-Coding Framework 41–5
Figure 5.4: Twelve Themes that Emerged from the People of the Diocese 46
Figure 5.5: Synod Voting Results 48
Figure 18.1: Example of Results Displayed during the Synod 107
Figure 18.2: Synod Voting Levels 108
Figure 18.3: Weighting of Votes 109
Figure 18.4: Community and Sense of Belonging – Total Score 111

Introduction

Karen Kiely and Éamonn Fitzgibbon

IN SEPTEMBER 2014, BISHOP BRENDAN LEAHY announced his intention to hold a diocesan synod by means of a pastoral letter entitled 'Together in Mission: A Time to Begin Again'. He invited all of us to go together on a *camino*, an appropriate metaphor since the word 'synod' means 'journeying together' or literally 'with someone on the road'.

As anyone who has walked the famous Camino de Santiago de Compostela knows, you can plan and study maps and guides but the way is still somewhat unknown and the path is only truly made by walking. Pilgrims on the Camino quickly learn that they need to be able to let go of many things and truly travel light. One has to be willing to ask for direction. While the arrival into Santiago de Compostela (or wherever one's destination may be) is always the goal, the journey is in many ways more important than the destination. Companionship along the way (even when walking alone) is extremely important. Finally the route can seem long and arduous and, if viewed in its entirety, daunting or even impossible – but day by day one moves forward, consoled with the thought, 'I am where I need to be for now.'

Similarly, on a synod journey one needs to make the path by walking, step by step. One needs to be willing to seek direction and guidance and recognise that this is a shared journey; one does not walk this way alone but with others. We may have to let go of many things – expectations or plans, for example – and trust in God's Spirit and the wisdom of other wayfarers and wise guides. At the end of our particular synod journey we are struck by the truly transformative effect that this journey has had on us all.

We offer this book, which is a series of short articles reflecting on various aspects of the Limerick Synod, as an aid and encouragement to the Irish Church as it embarks on a synodal pathway. It is important to note that many of the submissions were made immediately after the synod and, therefore, before it was known that the Irish Church would announce its own synodal process. The Irish Episcopal Conference has indicated that the initial two-year phase coinciding with preparation for the Ordinary General Assembly of Bishops in Rome entitled, 'For a Synodal Church: Communion, Participation and Mission' will consist of a period of prayer, listening and discernment, involving a nationwide consultative conversation on this theme. This will allow individuals and parishes, religious orders and associations as well as groups, movements and organisations, both within the Church and in Irish society at large, to share insights into the Church in Ireland – past, present and future. A planning and preparation phase for a national synodal assembly or assemblies will follow, bringing together and seeking to implement the fruits and recommendations from the initial phase.

It is our hope that our experience in Limerick will, in some way, inform the Irish Church at the threshold of this exciting moment in its history.

PART ONE: SETTING OUT

CHAPTER ONE
Together on the Way: Pope Francis and Synodality
Éamonn Fitzgibbon

GERRY O'HANLON HAS SAID THAT POPE FRANCIS IS leading a quiet revolution in the Church by means of a synodal approach.[1] In fact I am convinced that Francis' approach can only be understood through the lens of synodality and he is inviting us into a deeper understanding of all that this implies. Francis has said, 'The path of synodality is the path that God expects from the Church in the third millennium' and 'Synodality, as a constitutive dimension of the Church, offers us the best interpretative framework for understanding her hierarchical ministry.'[2] Indeed I would argue that synodality is also the best interpretative framework for understanding Francis' papacy. In fact, it is likely that we are being led to places that would not

---

1. Gerry O'Hanlon SJ, 'Ireland and the Quiet Revolution', *The Furrow*, Vol. LXVIII, No. 5 (May 2017), pp. 259–67.
2. Pope Francis, 'On the occasion of the fiftieth anniversary of the institution of the Synod of Bishops, the Holy Father addressed the Synod Fathers in the Vatican's Paul VI Hall', Vatican City, 19 October 2015 (VIS).

be Francis' personal preference, but if we are truly synodal we are often asked to hand over control to God, laying our own personal preferences to one side and allowing ourselves to be led in often surprising ways. In Santa Marta Francis said:

> And the way the Church expresses its communion is through synodality, by meeting, listening, debating, praying and deciding. The Spirit is always the protagonist and the Lord asks us not to be afraid when the Spirit calls us. ... Let us ask the Lord for grace to understand how the Church can face the surprises of the Spirit, to be docile and to follow the path which Christ wants for us and for the whole Church.[3]

At the heart of synodality is a sense of journey – of being on the road together – but the Greek word meaning 'journey', *hodos*, can also be understood as the more symbolically open 'way'; we are all on the way and followers of the Way. This image of Church as a community travelling together along the same road is congruent with one of the most powerful images of Church from the Second Vatican Council, which speaks of the Church as a pilgrim people, exiles journeying in a foreign land (*LG*, 6), but aware that the Lord walks with us so that we are led by the Spirit (*GS*, 11).

I had personal experience of this throughout our synod process in Limerick. Many of the clichés that can seem glib or trite were indeed proved true – the path was indeed made by walking. As the process unfolded, the diocesan synod evolved,

---

3. Pope Francis, 'Pope: There is always resistance in the Church to surprises of the Spirit', Vatican Radio, 28 April 2016, http://www.archivioradiovaticana.va/storico/2016/04/28/pope_there_is_always_resistance_to_surprises_of_the_spirit/en-1226132

working itself out over time and not in a prescriptive, overly managed or planned way. We learned to trust in the Spirit and cooperate and trust in the journey itself.

I believe that the synodal approach of Francis is most clearly evident in the Synod on the Family. The entire process bore the hallmarks of genuine synodality. In a sense the Synod on the Family could be described as a test case for the synodal way, particularly when we consider that it confronts us with difficult and complex issues, bringing us to those particular situations in family life where Church teaching and pastoral application meet. Francis himself referenced this when he said, 'From Vatican Council II to the current Synod Assembly on the family, we have experienced in an increasingly intense way the beauty of "walking together". … We must continue on this road.'[4] Francis listened, discerned, took on board the recommendations and spoke of the consensus of the Synod Fathers. The synodal way demanded that he walk a sometimes very fine line between two extremes.

If I could again reference our experience in Limerick of a diocesan synod, it is to Bishop Brendan Leahy's credit that he enabled – indeed, insisted on – an open and real listening, a listening in which nothing was off limits or out of bounds, in which all voices could be expressed and heard. Within the formal structure that is a synod this required courage and creativity. It also required honesty with delegates as the process moved towards the event itself:

> It will be important as we move through the process to tell all the people and especially the synod delegates what the limits are. If things are off limits for discussion (women's

---

4. Pope Francis, 'On the occasion of the fiftieth anniversary of the institution of the Synod of Bishops'.

ordination, clerical celibacy, the cathedraticum) we must say so up front and not raise unfounded hopes. People can deal with limits if we tell them the right way. They cannot deal with the promise of wide horizons and then the stifling of their most creative conclusions.[5]

And yet, we found creative ways that enabled us to stretch the boundaries of what is possible within the legal requirements of a valid synod, which were not censorial or restrictive. This is the synodal way of Francis; it allows for the *parresia* that he has called for, the courage to speak openly and plainly even if it is a contrarian view. On the final day of our synod gathering in Limerick, space was created to allow such open and frank discussion. The respectful manner in which delegates spoke and listened on matters that were deeply felt, and with differing viewpoints deeply held, spoke volumes to the journey that all of us delegates had been on – a journey that had brought us to this place of *parresia*.

Listening

At the heart of any synod and synodal method is deep listening:

> A Synodal Church is a Church which listens, aware that listening is more than hearing. It is a process of mutual listening in which each person has something to learn. The faithful, the Episcopal College, the Bishop of Rome: each one listening to the others, and all listening to the Holy Spirit, the 'Spirit of truth.'[6]

---

5. Ann F. Rehrauer, 'The Diocesan Synod', CLSA Proceedings of the Forty-Ninth Annual Convention, Washington DC: Canon Law Society of America, 1987, 14.

6. Pope Francis, 'On the occasion of the fiftieth anniversary of the institution of the Synod of Bishops'.

Pope Francis is building on the call of Vatican II to listen to the 'sense of the faithful' recognising the Spirit speaking through God's people:

> The People of God believes that it is led by the Spirit of the Lord, who fills the earth. Motivated by this faith, it labours to decipher authentic signs of God's presence and purpose in the happenings, needs, and desires in which this People has a part along with others of our age. (*GS*, 11)

In Limerick, we used a variety of listening methods in a lengthy listening process that heard from approximately five thousand people. The fruit of this open listening was coded and subsequently thematised, which in turn generated the 101 proposals brought to the synod floor. The listening revealed that the most important issues in people's lives centre on relationships – family, community and young people. In choosing 'Family' as the theme for his first Synod of Bishops and 'Young People' as his second, Francis clearly demonstrates his sensitivity to what is truly important to people.

Process over Event, Time over Space
In *Evangelii Gaudium* Francis gave us the intriguing and complex phrase: 'Time is greater than space' (*EG*, 222–5). This reminds us that in a truly synodal experience, the process is more important than the programme, the journey is greater than the destination, the lead-in more critical than the event. It is too easy to plan an event, a quick-win, eye-catching moment that quickly withers away and leaves little impact. We would do well to heed Francis' warning to generate 'processes of people-building, as opposed to obtaining immediate results which yield easy, quick short-term political gains, but do not enhance human fullness' (*EG*,

224). The phrase reminds us also that there is often a gap or a space between where we might like to be (the ideal) and where we are at in reality but time is greater than that space too and it can be bridged over time. It is not about dominating spaces but about keeping an eye on the end-goal, 'the horizon which constantly opens before us' (*EG*, 222). Francis also tells us that 'realities are more important than ideas' (*EG*, 231–3) and each of these somewhat obscure phrases ('Time is greater than space' and 'Realities are more important than ideas') find very practical expression in the grounded situations of family life in *Amoris Laetitia*.

In Limerick our experience taught us that the process itself is transformative as it provides an opportunity for genuine participation, consultation, and formation. It is a moment of evangelisation for a diocese as it embraces this time of prayerful discernment and catechesis: 'If the members of the diocese are properly engaged in a participatory process, [this can] also result in broad-based renewal.'[7]

Discernment

In a synodal process, discernment is essential and, as a Jesuit, Francis is very aware of the importance of this. Christian discernment is not about figuring out and choosing what I want but rather it is about discerning God's will for my life and thus involves attentive listening to the Spirit's guidance. Twenty times discernment was mentioned in *Evangelii Gaudium* and it is a hallmark of Francis' synodal approach. In his letter to the bishops of Buenos Aires on *Amoris Laetitia*, Francis said, 'It simply entails accepting, accompanying, discerning, reinstating. Out of these four pastoral attitudes the least refined and practised

---

7. Barbara A. Cusack, 'The Diocesan Synod: A Teachable Moment in the Life of the Local Church', *The Jurist*, 63, 2003, p. 73.

is discernment; and I deem it urgent to include training in personal and community discernment in our Seminaries and Presbyteries.'[8] It is fair to say that most of us have not received adequate training to develop skills of discernment.

Conclusion

Alongside his teaching on time being greater than space is Francis' understanding of the law of gradualness (as opposed to the gradualness of law). We are journeying within a culture of mercy (*AL*, 295). The synodal way is difficult but Pope Francis has invited us to walk with him on a journey. He has shown us that together we can find a new way.

---

8. Pope Francis, 'Letter of the Holy Father to the Bishops of Buenos Aires', 5 September 2016.

CHAPTER TWO
Convoking a Synod
Bishop Brendan Leahy

I HAVE OFTEN BEEN ASKED – WHY DID I CALL A SYNOD? The most immediate reason was that when I became bishop of Limerick, I quickly realised the diocese had already engaged in a valuable and widespread listening exercise under the wise guidance of Bishop Donal Murray and had taken many positive steps in developing clusters and pastoral areas. I had to build on that not repeat it. If you don't go forward, you go backwards. Added to that, with all the painful difficulties that the Church in Ireland has been going through, including the diocese, I felt a collective step was needed. A synod seemed to fit that bill.

I had many other reasons. As a Church activity, a synod is a time-honoured and well-thought-out organised process that listens to the heartbeat of a diocese and indicates precise directions that can then become local Church law. A synod is a way of taking up the gospel's invitation to work more in unity with one another. Pope Francis has emphasised the importance of synods in the Church. My theological studies had convinced me of the value of promoting what might be called a synodal style in the Church.[1]

Questions before a Synod

Before the official act of convocation, a bishop is bound to consult widely. I did so with various groups – the College of Consultors, the Priests' Council, lay members of the pastoral areas and others. They gave me positive approval for the initiative.

Admittedly, some suggested the word 'synod' was odd. Maybe we should call the process something else. I believed, however, that while the term has fallen into disuse, it's still a word worth recuperating. Not just the word but, more importantly, the practice of holding synods.

There's an element of risk in convoking a synod. Years ago, a diocesan synod was mostly a matter of just a morning, or a day or two's deliberations, with the bishop and some clergy making practical decisions. To convoke a synod today is different. It is more about process and dialogue. And just like when any of us start talking about anything, it can take time to sort out our viewpoints and what we want to say and where we are going with it all. A synod is a process during which people express hopes and wishes, but also fears and anxieties. There's a risk that some might take personally comments intended on a more general level.

Then there are the issues that go beyond a bishop's specific diocesan remit. Will hot-button issues get disproportionate coverage, distracting from the real everyday concerns of people? Will media coverage focus on just the controversial issues?

---

1. See Brendan Leahy, 'People, Synod and Upper Room: Vatican II's Ecclesiology of Communion' in Dermot A. Lane and Brendan Leahy (eds), *Vatican II: Facing the 21st Century*, Dublin: Veritas, 2006, pp. 49–80.

Finally, there is the question of cost. It was said to me, however, that while we so often have to spend a lot of money on Church buildings, it is wise to spend money on a synod that constructs the building that is the Church, the People of God.

In reflecting on these issues, I also learned from the experiences of synods in America and Rome. The 1997 Vatican *Instruction on Diocesan Synods* was an important resource.

The Pastoral Letter

In convoking the synod in September 2014, I issued a pastoral letter entitled, 'Together in Mission: A Time to Begin Again'. As well as outlining the reasons for the synod and explaining some of the steps involved, I indicated how I wanted to make my own the words of Pope Francis in his apostolic letter *Evangelii Gaudium*, on the joy of the gospel: 'I dream of a "missionary option", that is, a missionary impulse capable of transforming everything, so that the Church's customs, ways of doing things, times and schedules, language and structures can be suitably channelled for the evangelisation of today's world rather than for her self-preservation' (27).

I recounted how I often heard people in Limerick talk about the 'Miracle Match', a great day back in 2003, when Munster, against all the odds, by determination, by working together, and above all by having a dream, advanced to the semi-finals of the Heineken Cup. I expressed the hope that if we would work together with a new enthusiasm, we, too, could advance as a Church.

I explained that I didn't want to predetermine the outcomes, nevertheless, I indicated pitfalls to avoid: firstly, focusing just on structures; secondly, limiting ourselves to our own local experience without looking at the bigger picture; thirdly, narrowing our vision to specifically religious or liturgical questions rather than looking at the social dimensions of the

Church. I felt it was important too to emphasise that for the synod to be successful it would need to touch each one of us personally and spiritually. We were entering a period of spiritual 'discernment'.

What to Expect
Some say to me that I had courage to call a synod. I don't see it like that. It was simply the right thing to do – the Risen Jesus would lead us when gathered in his name, in love for one another. I think I received a grace to believe in the process of the synod as linked to the Holy Spirit. In all of this, I tried to keep before me the figure of the Crucified Christ, who in difficulty and even apparent failure generated the Church, and so I thought to myself: even if it goes badly, it'll go okay.

CHAPTER THREE
Journeying Towards the Synod
Éamonn Fitzgibbon

A SYNOD IS BOTH A PROCESS AND AN EVENT. THIS IS why 'journey' is such a powerful metaphor (two words, *syn hodos*, that mean 'with [someone]' and 'road'). A journey places equal emphasis on the travelling as the destination. Theologically, 'journey' is also a rich image; it conveys the sense of a community travelling together. *Lumen Gentium* speaks of the Church as a pilgrim people. Spiritually, we see in 'journey' participation, dialogue, discernment and renewal, all guided by the Holy Spirit. It is impossible to overstate the importance of prayer, for in a diocesan synod the work must be God's work or it will remain 'much ado about nothing'.

The guidance for this journey – because it is a formal Church structure – is contained in the *Code of Canon Law* (Canons 460–8) and subsequently in the *Instruction on Diocesan Synods* (Congregation for Bishops, 23 October 1997). As the Diocese of Limerick began its preparations, it also learned from the experience of synods in other parts of the world. It was important that all delegates and, indeed, the wider community were aware from the outset that a synod is not deliberative but rather a consultative body recommending to the bishop, who is the sole legislator, a direction for the future.

The *Instruction* requires the bishop to establish a preparatory commission whose responsibility it is to oversee the organisation and delivery of the synod. A preparatory commission of over twenty members was put in place to oversee the process. The next step was to identify and recruit delegates – these delegates must be drawn from a wide base so as to be truly reflective of the face of the diocese. We successfully recruited four hundred delegates from parishes and communities across the diocese who truly reflect the diversity and richness of our diocesan community. The synod was formally convoked in December 2014. The commitment and enthusiasm of the delegates was striking. They freely gave up their time to attend various in-service and formation events; they carried out synod tasks in their own communities in a way that was characterised by enthusiasm and optimism.

The time between the convocation of a synod and the synod itself is primarily a time of discerning the agenda. The time allowed needs to be such that there is time for real discernment and reflection. The delegates carried out the enormous task of listening to their own communities – using a variety of methods to discern the hopes and fears, the joys and sorrows of the people with whom they live and work. Delegates needed to be supported and trained in the skills necessary to carry out such listening – a listening that bears the hallmark of true Christian discernment under the guidance of the Holy Spirit.

The parish delegates were tasked with gathering views and ideas from parishioners and groups in a range of ways – parish meetings, focus groups, questionnaires (some five thousand replied to the questionnaires) and school inputs. Subsequently, the delegates discerned and selected the themes which would be brought forward to the synod.

Journeying Towards the Synod

Along the way we have had wonderful gatherings. We held meetings with young adults and second-level school students. I am thinking in particular of the initial, introductory gathering in the Lime Tree Theatre with Fr Paul Philibert, a US-based Dominican theologian who has written wonderfully on lay ministry and the priesthood of the faithful. Father Paul challenged us to be agents and not clients in the Church. (Sadly Fr Paul died on 14 April 2016 just a few days after the conclusion of our synod on 10 April.) We held an orientation day in January 2015 in the Radisson, a review in Thomond Park in June, and a prayerful reflective day of discernment in October 2015 in the Strand Hotel when the six synod themes were selected.

The synod has truly been a from-the-ground-up journey, whereby the experience of the people in our parishes and communities has been recognised as the place of God's presence and the Spirit's voice. It has been a genuine attempt to model theological reflection, whereby the experience of people – gleaned from the listening process in the spring of 2015 – has been put into dialogue with aspects of our tradition – through catechesis on baptism and Eucharist, through Bishop Brendan's pastoral on Vatican II or his helpful text on praying the Acts of the Apostles.

In journeying towards the synod, we welcomed Níall McLaughlin, the renowned architect, and Sir Harry Burns, the former chief medical officer for Scotland. Of course, there has also been the interaction with many people locally who have acted as wise guides to us on the journey – people like Niamh Hourigan, John Weafer, Gerry O'Hanlon SJ, Jessie Rogers, Rosemary O'Connor and many others. We were privileged to benefit from the input of Bishop Kenneth Kearon, the then bishop of Limerick and Killaloe in the Church of Ireland. Similarly, Jerry O'Dea, then mayor of Limerick City, addressed the synod gathering representing the civic community. Perhaps of greatest importance was the planning and reflection with Martin Kennedy, our local prophet to his own land. One does not travel alone on the pilgrim path and we were fortunate that we had the members of the Preparatory Commission and these local facilitators and trainers who were hugely important on the road.

In the Diocese of Limerick we have so many wonderful resources available to us, none more so than the resource that is Mary Immaculate College. The Department of Theology and Religious Studies contributed greatly to the time of preparation and, of course, the synod event itself took place in the College – as did a number of the events leading to April 2016. We were involved in a very interesting project with the Geography Department at Mary Immaculate College. Doctors Brendan O'Keeffe and Shane O'Sullivan mapped the findings of the 2011 census to our parishes. Considering that the CSO and the parishes have two differing boundaries, this was no small task but it meant that we now had a very good sense of who our parishes are. We could know with strong accuracy how many people live in each parish, their age, education, employment, gender, affluence or poverty levels, religious affiliation, family make-up, etc. It is the final piece in the three-way conversation of a genuine theological reflection, bringing in context or culture to the dialogue. For me personally it has been a joy to work with and watch these social geographers plying their trade. Indeed, it has been one part of a much wider engagement by the Church in the wider world.

That positive engagement with the wider world is congruent with a position whereby the synod process recognises God's activity in the world. This brings to mind a gathering titled 'Limerick: What is our Mission?' that was attended by representatives of private business, local government, arts, sports and political circles – a range of city- and county-based stakeholders. The Church needs to be in constant conversation with the wider world and this event explored what Limerick's identity for the future could be and the role the Catholic Church might have to play in developing this. The synod must not be overly 'churchy' in a narrow sense; it must not become inward looking but be truly missionary, reaching out and looking to the community at large. We recognise God's activity in so many situations and are part of a shift whereby we might be less preoccupied with getting people back into the Church as becoming preoccupied with going out to where people are living out their lives.

CHAPTER FOUR
Preparing the Way: The Preparatory Commission

Shane Ambrose

> 'Any committee that is the slightest use is composed of people who are too busy to want to sit on it for a second longer than they have to.' (Katharine Whitehorn)

AN EVENT OF THE MAGNITUDE OF A DIOCESAN SYNOD is not one that the normal structures of a diocesan administration would manage successfully and one of the first requirements that any bishop planning to convoke a diocesan synod is required to do is to establish a preparatory commission to assist with the specific preparation of the synod.[1] The membership of the commission is selected by the bishop and brings together a spectrum of people from across the diocese who, as far as possible, 'reflect the various charisms and ministries of the People of God'.[2]

One of the initial tasks given to the Limerick Diocesan Synod Preparatory Commission (LDSPC) was to identify and recruit

---

1. Congregation for Bishops, *Instruction on Diocesan Synods*, 23 October 1997, III, B, 1.
2. *Instruction*, III, B, 1.

delegates who would attend the synod event in 2016.[3] This rapidly expanded to helping with the organisation and preparation of the pre-synod training and discernment, and then to assist with the actual synod event itself.

While the LDSPC had twenty-four members, for effectiveness it operated a number of subcommissions into which others outside the core group were co-opted to provide technical and specialist support.[4] The LDSPC was separate to the Secretariat, which also held the responsibility of coordinating synodal communication, archiving and event management; however, it was necessary to have a great deal of coordination and dual membership between the two.

The LDSPC operated in plenary once a month as the Consultative Commission of the Synod to the Bishop. One of the first challenges for the LDSPC was to scope out its own role during the whole process. Each synodal event has its own unique character and the specific role of the preparatory commission can vary from diocese to diocese and there isn't a step-by-step guide for preparatory commissions. The experience of the LDSPC was very much a journey mirroring the overall *camino* of the synod itself: we were creating the way as we walked. One of the key things for the LDSPC was the recognition that the synod process is a process of discernment and that we must reflect this in our openness to listening and recognising where the Spirit of God was guiding us. It did raise the question of how we could ensure that there was good listening within LDSPC itself, with the delegates, with people across the diocese and in how

---

3. Bishop Brendan Leahy, 'Together in Mission: A Time to Begin Again' (pastoral letter), 2014, 2.
4. 'Members of the Preparatory Commission', *Synod2016*, http://www.synod2016.com/what-is-a-synod/members-of-the-preparatory-commission/

Preparing the Way: The Preparatory Commission

we filtered information back to people and parishes. Someone described the delegates as our 'hunter-gatherers', and we needed to explore the ways in which we could help them.

The subcommissions of the LDSPC included:
- Spiritual and Catechetical Subcommission, which undertook to draw up and roll out the spiritual formation of both the delegates and the wider diocese in the synodal process and what it meant.
- Liturgy Subcommission (included a separate group coordinating a synodal hymn), which coordinated the various liturgical events throughout the preparatory phase of the synod and the prayer moments and formal liturgies of the synod itself in April 2016.
- Legal Subcommission (canonical and civil), which focused on drawing up the synodal directory[5] and ensuring that matters raised and discussed by the synod fell within the competence of diocesan oversight, and post synod to draw up the formal synodal decrees for the *recognitio* and promulgation by the Bishop.
- Youth Subcommission, whose role was to ensure that issues of concern to *an eaglais óg* were voiced and included in the synod. Thus, a separate group was tasked with coordinating specific events to gather the input of the young church to the discussions of the synod.
- Statistical Analysis and Data Processing Subcommission, which was a key group in the overall synod process. Due to the fact that the issues and topics to be discussed were surfaced from various groups throughout the diocese, as part of the synod preparation process that information had to be organised, analysed and presented in such a

---

5. 'Synod Directory', *Synod2016*, http://www.synod2016.com/what-is-a-synod/synodal-directory/

way that could be utilised by the delegates during their deliberations. This group in particular drew on the skills and resources available throughout the diocese and, in particular, in Mary Immaculate College in terms of using best practice for research methodology.

The process of the LDSPC was extensive and required real commitment to the synod process. But it was also an uplifting event for members as it provided an insight into the variety and diversity of the diocese, the way ordinary people are living out their faith in their day-to-day lives and how important that faith is to them. It also highlighted the challenges that the institutional Church poses in terms of outreach and openness to the space where people are at.

PART TWO: ON THE WAY

Chapter Five
Listening: A Process Involving Many
Rosemary O'Connor

'The ear of the leader must ring with the voices of the people.' (Woodrow Wilson)

THE SYNOD PREPARATION JOURNEY INVOLVED AN extensive listening process that took place from February to October 2015. Figure 5.1 illustrates the timeline of the four phases that brought the synod delegates through a listening and discernment process in their respective communities, a data coding and analysis phase that engaged a group of research experts and a data analysis group, a sifting process that identified a long list of possible synod themes, and then finally a selection process that resulted in the six themes that formed the synod agenda and ultimately shaped the diocesan pastoral plan.

Listening and Discernment
A training programme to enhance listening and facilitation skills was offered to all four hundred synod delegates. The training offered in four geographic locations throughout the diocese presented eight different methods for pastoral listening and discernment. Figure 5.2 illustrates the eight models.

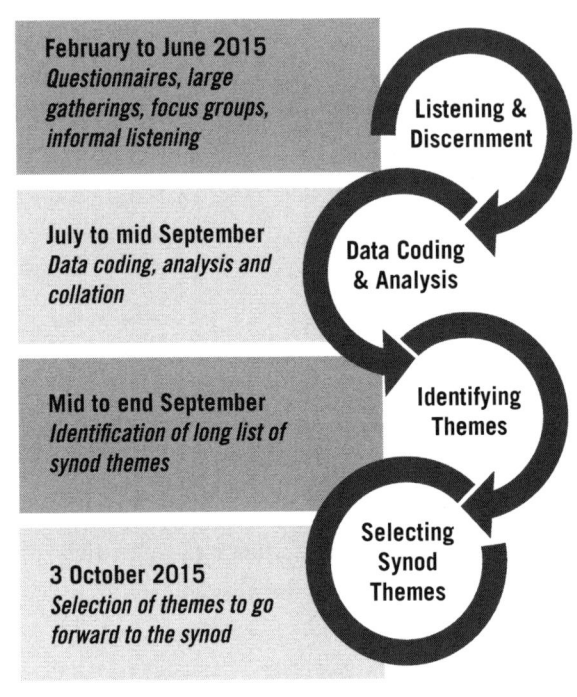

Figure 5.1: Timeline of the Four Phases

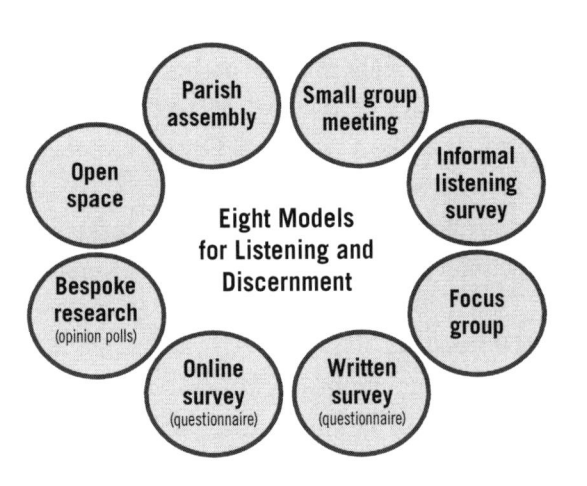

Figure 5.2: Eight Models for Listening and Discernment

Listening: A Process Involving Many

Delegates were invited to select the listening and discernment models that best suited their local needs. Regardless of the model(s) selected, the same three questions were asked throughout the process:
1. What are the topics that you would like to see on the agenda for the Limerick Diocesan Synod in 2016?
2. a) What is it that encourages you to participate in the life of your local Church?
   b) What is it that you find difficult about participating in your local Church?
3. Where, in your everyday life, do you experience love, truth, goodness, hope and joy?

The questions were intended to draw out people's positive and negative experiences of Church and to identify where the Holy Spirit is at work in the diocese. All sixty parishes in the diocese participated in the listening and discernment process, as well as twenty-five other groups that included primary, secondary and third-level education, the Traveller community, healthcare, the Polish community, people with disabilities, social workers, youth ministry groups and several faith-related and religious groups. More than four thousand people filled in questionnaires and a further over one thousand five hundred people participated in large gatherings and small-group discussions. There was emphasis placed on trying to reach people on the fringes and outside of our faith communities, those that have lost connection with or become disenfranchised from the Church. In many parishes, innovative approaches were adopted to engage with young people through sports clubs and youth clubs. In one parish the delegates set up a stand in a busy shopping centre and canvassed the views of the public as they passed through.

Data Coding and Analysis

In order to do justice to the extensive work undertaken by the delegates and the large data set arising from the four thousand plus questionnaires and the sixty reports from the group discussions, a group of research experts were invited to share their perspectives on how best to handle the data. Their expertise ranged from scripture and theology to discernment to social research. The research experts included Dr Jessie Rogers, Dr Eugene Duffy, Bishop Donal Murray, Dr Niamh Hourigan, Dr John Weafer and Fr Gerry Clarke SJ. The research experts debated amongst themselves how they would approach the data coding and analysis task. Following dialogue with the team of fifteen data analysts, a number of key guiding principles emerged:

- The data analysis process should be grounded in a discernment approach that creates a prayerful environment and cultivates a sense of openness and freedom that allows the voices of the people to be heard.
- Careful attention should be paid to the 'still small voices' in the collective and the individual. Views that grated or irritated should be noted to ensure they are not lost.
- The data should be reviewed across all three questions asked to get a comprehensive perspective of the views of the people and facilitate the key topics to emerge.
- A ground-up inductive approach should be adopted by taking a sample from right across the data set and then analysing it to determine what codes emanated from the data. In this way, a data-coding framework that emerged from the data itself was established. The coding framework had twenty-three codes and 153 subcodes.

A group of fifteen data analysts worked on the data over the course of the summer of 2015, sorting the data into the coding framework. The codes and subcodes were used to label and organise the data; a simple analogy would be the organisation of thousands of documents into a filing cabinet with multiple drawers that are further subdivided into smaller sections. The data-coding framework is laid out below in Figure 5.3 (pp. 41–5).

A mixed method approach, using both quantitative and qualitative methodologies, was adopted to analyse the data by extracting quantitative data (i.e. the frequency with which certain codes were mentioned) and qualitative data (i.e. extracting quotations from the data to add depth and colour to the numbers and to effectively tell the story).

CODE 1: COMMUNITY
- Parish
  - Community
  - Building
  - A new sense of
- Social dimension
- Welcome
  - Tea/coffee after Mass
- Sense of belonging or lack of belonging
- 'Cliques' formed
- Social space (young people)
- Caring ethos
- Reducing Mass times
- Shared beliefs

CODE 2: CLERGY
- Ageing profile
- Married
- Inclusion or readmission of former clergy
- Shortage of
- Pastoral care of
- Vocations
- Homilies
- Permanent diaconate
- Personal skills and enthusiasms

CODE 3: LAITY
- Governance
- More education and training
- Leadership roles
- Empowering of youth
- Time poverty

- Remuneration
- Voluntary options
- Clear roles
- Invitation to participate
- Work as Christian life
- Lay involvement

CODE 4: ROLE OF WOMEN
- Vocation (multi-layered)
- Leadership
  - More involvement in decision-making
- Deaconate role for women
- Ordination of women
- Tokenism
- Sexist language in the liturgy

CODE 5: YOUTH
- Disenfranchised
- Confirmation
  - Graduation from Church
- Inclusion of youth in local church
  - Active roles
  - Participation
- Safeguarding
- Language
  - Accessible
- Dialogue with youth
- Choices around faith
- Experience of liturgy
  - Old-fashioned
  - Boring
- Youth clubs
  - Connection outside of church
- Youth ministry

CODE 6: CHILDREN
- Mindset towards *Do This in Memory*
- More involvement
- Liturgy for children
  - Including Masses and child-friendly prayers
- Sacramental preparation
- Role of parents/guardians as religious educators
- Religion in the home
- Sunday school
- Care of children with learning difficulties
- Supportive adults

CODE 7: LEADERSHIP
- Governance
- Roles
  - Of priest: spiritual leader vs administrator
  - Of laity
- Formation and training of leaders
  - Laity
  - Clergy
- Support from leadership
- Different models of leadership
  - Preparing for a different future reality
- Witness
- Pope's rallying call for renewal

CODE 8: LITURGY AND PRAYER
- Joyful and life-giving
  - Especially Easter and Christmas
- Format
- Music
- Church environment
- Relevant homilies
- Rubrics
- New Missal
- Ritual – special moments in life
- Going through the motions – congregation
- Time
  - Length of celebration
- Creative liturgies or new ways of praying
- Hearing the word of God
- Times of Masses
- Prayer at home
- Ecumenical services
- Bible studies, prayer group, discussion groups on noticeboard

CODE 9: SACRAMENTS
- Confession
  - General absolution
- Understanding emphasis
- Links in sacramental preparation: hymns used in parish not just for the day
  - Home
  - School
  - Parish
- Age of Confirmation and Communion
- Children to apply to be confirmed
- Confirmation and Holy Communion in children's home parish

CODE 10: CATECHESIS
- How to live the Gospel
- Adult faith formation
- The Ten Commandments
- Use of catechism in primary school
- RE in primary/post-primary schools
- Catechism in liturgy
- Scripture/Bible study

CODE 11: SPIRITUALITY
- Meditation/reflection
- Mindfulness
- Special moments
  - Dawn Mass
- Personal prayer
- Adoration
- Multi-denominational experience

CODE 12: CATHOLIC EDUCATION
- Ethos of Catholic school
- Relevance to young people

CODE 13: DISCONNECTED FROM THE CHURCH
- Young people
- Declining numbers
- Church language
- Church teaching vs lived reality
- People on the margins
- Voicelessness of people on the margins
- Lack of trust
- Clergy disconnected from modern life
- Enforced conformity

CODE 14: CAUSES OF ALIENATION FROM THE CHURCH
- Contraception
- Teaching on sexuality
- People in second relationships/divorced
- LGBT
- Abortion

CODE 15: SOCIAL JUSTICE

CODE 16: CHURCH IN THE MODERN WORLD
- Social media
- Not knowing role of Church in a secular society

Listening: A Process Involving Many

CODE 17: COMPASSION
- LGBT community
- Suicide
- Financial difficulties
- Unexpected pregnancies
- Pastoral care of disabled, elderly, terminally ill and people in need

CODE 18: RELATIONSHIPS
- Family
- Friends
- Work colleagues
- Children
- Students
- Volunteers
- Community

CODE 19: INTERFAITH
- Dialogue with other faith traditions

CODE 20: COMMUNICATIONS
- Different media
- Newsletter
- Active listening

CODE 21: FINANCES
- Diocesan needs commission
- Accountability and transparency around finances

CODE 22: ISSUES
- Church response to wrongdoings
- Church-gate collections
- Mental health
- Gay marriage and equality for gay people
- Mass cards – name of deceased not recorded
- Gluten-free hosts

CODE 23: OTHER VOICES
- Issues of trust
- Nature, including animals
- Music
- Sport
- Work
- Good health
- Positive responses around faith

Figure 5.3: Data-Coding Framework

Identifying Themes

The next step in the process was to move codes to themes; whilst the codes are used to sort and organise the data, a theme presents a phrase or sentence that identifies what the data means; essentially it makes sense of the codes and identifies the key topics contained in the data. This involved an analysis and sieving of the coded data to arrive at a set of themes. This sieving process resulted in the identification of twelve themes that reflected the key topics of relevance and concern to the people of the diocese. Figure 5.4 illustrates the twelve themes that emerged.

```
  ( Parish    )  ( Other      )  ( Social     )
  (  data     )  ( groups'    )  ( partner    )
                 (  data      )  (  data      )
                    ┌─────────┐
                    │ THEMES  │
                    └─────────┘
```

Care for the Earth	Community and Sense of Belonging
Faith Formation, Education, Catechesis	Healing Hurts
Liturgy and Life	Ministry Roles
New Models of Pastoral Leadership – *Facing the New Reality*	Pastoral Care of the Family
Social Justice	Spirituality and Ways of Praying
Women in the Church	Young People

Figure 5.4: Twelve Themes that Emerged from the People of the Diocese

Selecting Synod Themes

On 3 October 2015, a full gathering of synod delegates was held where the twelve themes were presented using both quantitative and qualitative data. The delegates were guided through a discernment exercise to reflect on the voices of the people and what they had said. Each delegate was invited to rank the twelve themes in what they felt was the correct order of priority from one to twelve using a ranking sheet.

A team of data analysts inputted the data from each of the ranking sheets to an Excel spreadsheet with pre-coded formulae. The formulae applied a weighting system to the ranking, which assigned a score of twelve to the theme that was ranked as number one, a score of eleven to the theme ranked as number two and so on right down to a score of one being assigned to the theme ranked as number twelve on each of the delegate's ranking sheets. This resulted in a global ranking of the twelve themes by combining the rankings provided by the individual delegates. Figure 5.5 illustrates the results of the global ranking of the twelve themes by all delegates; the figures indicated are the total scores for each theme. The six themes chosen to form the agenda of the synod itself are highlighted.

The six themes selected formed the agenda for Synod 2016:
1. Community and Sense of Belonging
2. Faith Formation, Education, Catechesis
3. Pastoral Care of the Family
4. New Models of Pastoral Leadership
5. Liturgy and Life
6. Young People

Topic	Votes
Community and Sense of Belonging	2413
Faith Formation, Education, Catechesis	2346
Pastoral Care of the Family	2178
New Models of Pastoral Leadership	2148
Liturgy and Life	2013
Young People	1862
Ministry Roles	1545
Women in the Church	1503
Healing Hurts	1480
Spirituality and Ways of Praying	1444
Social Justice	1387
Care for the Earth	1147

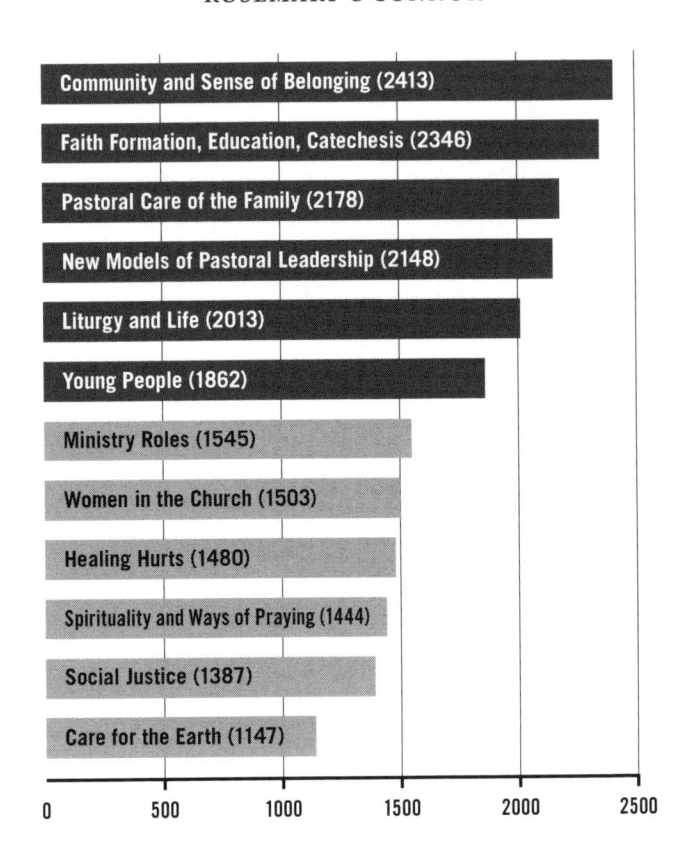

Figure 5.5: Synod Voting Results

CHAPTER SIX

Discerning: Learning a New Art Together

Jessie Rogers

THE SYNOD JOURNEY, AT ITS HEART, HAS BEEN A JOURNEY of faith. It was built upon the conviction that this was not simply a human endeavour, but that somehow, in and through the process, God's Spirit was at work. These are the beliefs that anchored our approach:

- God is at work in the world and in the people and communities that make up the Diocese of Limerick. That work draws the world (and the diocese) in the direction of love and life and wholeness.
- The people of God, who have God's Spirit within and among them, are invited to work alongside God.
- God's people are able to hear and respond to God's invitation. God wants to transform our communities with the joy of the gospel even more than we do. So if we ask 'Does God want us to know how to go forward?' the answer is yes!
- The Spirit's invitation to the Church can be heard as we let God's Word shape our imagination, and by listening to our deepest (God-given) desires and to others, particularly those on the margins.

Believing these things called for discernment on the part of the delegates. Discernment is a decision-making process that actively seeks to align our spirits with God's Spirit. It is not a fuzzy affair – the delegates worked hard to become as well informed as possible. The listening process and input by various experts grounded them in reality and the catechetical opportunities helped them to bring their faith to bear on the facts and possibilities that emerged. There were experts to help with drafting of proposals. But we wanted our deliberations and decisions to be more than just the best research and thinking we were capable of. We wanted the process to be open to the Holy Spirit and to be led and inspired by God. So we introduced times of quiet and reflection in addition to more formal prayer times. Aware that we were in God's presence, we could also become aware as individuals of the movement of our own spirits in response to God's Spirit. We listened to ourselves. Delegates were asked to notice what resonated with them or made them feel hopeful, and also to notice what jarred or made them uneasy. Our own hopes and fears (individual and communal) and attachment to our own agendas can easily drown out the still small voice of the Spirit. But when people are still for a while in God's presence, the deeper God-given desires of their hearts begin to be heard. Then small-group discussion has the potential to go beyond an exercise in sharing opinions and become a way to listen together for the divine whisper.

Our journey was one of group discernment, which means that the delegates were listening to each other as well as to their own deep selves in order to catch what God might be saying. That careful, prayerful listening to what others said might confirm an individual's sense or conviction, but sometimes it might gently challenge or modify it. It is a delicate balance that requires respect and a high level of trust within the group. It isn't going to work unless the Spirit who brings unity within diversity is truly present and active. For some people the challenge was to find the courage to give voice to their own convictions, for others it was to listen with an openness to the possibility that their own deeply held position may be wrong. To facilitate that, we had times in small groups where delegates were encouraged to simply state their thoughts and feelings on the topic, not to argue or to try to convince others, and to listen in turn to what each person had to say. This was followed by a time of silent reflection on what had been heard, to give people an opportunity to notice again their own deep responses and how those may have been confirmed or shifted by what they heard. The discussion that followed that process had more potential to be inspired and insightful. None of this is easy, and it can go against the grain of how people characteristically interact in groups. So we would begin by stopping to consider what grace we each needed to ask God for. What did we need right now to engage well with *this* question or issue, with *these* people in the group?

Discernment was an integral part of our synodal journey. Did we 'get it right'? The process was not perfect, and we were learning as we went along. But that is probably not the right question to ask anyway. Was God with us, guiding and growing us? Did the spirit of the delegates respond to the promptings of the Spirit? Did the discussions and decisions move the diocese further along the path of gospel love and joy? I think so. A recurring experience at the synod that stays with me is the richness of the times of silence, which profoundly shaped the atmosphere and the tone of the whole endeavour. Those were God-filled silences. Of that I am sure.

CHAPTER SEVEN

The Synod in Canon Law

Gerard Garrett

THE DIOCESE OF LIMERICK IS 'A PORTION OF THE PEOPLE of God, which is entrusted to a bishop [Bishop Brendan Leahy] to be nurtured by him, with the cooperation of the presbyterium [priests of the diocese], in such a way that, remaining close to its pastor and gathered by him through the gospel and the Eucharist in the Holy Spirit, it constitutes a particular Church. In this Church, the one, holy, Catholic and Apostolic Church of Christ truly exists and functions.'[1] The bishops 'succeed the Apostles through the Holy Spirit who is given to them' and 'are constituted Pastors in the Church, to be the teachers of doctrine, the priests of sacred worship and the ministers of governance'.[2] In the fulfilment of these pastoral functions of his office, the diocesan bishop may and, indeed, ought to call upon the priests

---

1. *The Code of Canon Law* in English translation, prepared by the Canon Law Society of Great Britain and Ireland in association with the Canon Law Society of Australia and New Zealand and the Canadian Canon Law Society, London: Collins, 1983, can. 369.
2. *The Code of Canon Law*, can. 375 §1.

and people, lay and religious, to assist him. Through their common baptism, the Holy Spirit dwells in them. While many informal means of consultation are available to him, the formal, canonical manner of doing this is the diocesan synod.[3]

The Code of Canon Law contains 1752 canons yet merely nine of those are devoted to the topic of the diocesan synod; they are canons 460 to 468. These, however, are expanded upon by an *Instruction* of the Holy See, which provides what could be called a road map for the process that is a diocesan synod.[4] It is a process, and a lengthy one at that, because it involves the discernment, through prayer, catechesis, research, discussion and debate and finally consensus, of a considerable body of advice to the diocesan bishop. This advice is given to him so that he, exercising the charism proper to his office as diocesan bishop, can evaluate the existing pastoral initiatives in the diocese and to devise new pastoral initiatives for the future care of the diocese.

Once the synod is concluded and the bishop is in possession of this considerable body of advice, it is his responsibility to distil it, as it were, into a document comprising declarations and decrees. Only he has the authority to do this: 'The diocesan Bishop is the sole legislator in the diocesan synod. Other members of the synod have only a consultative vote. The diocesan Bishop alone signs the synodal declarations and decrees, and only by his authority may these be published.'[5]

The *Instruction* of the Holy See sets out the nature of the post-synodal declarations and decrees: 'By the terms "decrees"

---

3. There are some occasions when the diocesan bishop is required by law to consult certain persons and bodies and even to have the consent of certain persons and bodies before positing some juridic acts.
4. Congregation for Bishops, *Instruction on Diocesan Synods*, 1997.
5. *The Code of Canon Law*, can. 466.

and "declarations" the Code of Canon Law envisages the possibility that texts emanating from synods consist, on the one hand, of true juridic norms – that may be termed "constitutions" [or statutes] or otherwise – or directives for future pastoral programmes and, on the other, of opportune affirmations of the truth of the Catholic faith or morals, especially in relation to more important aspects of the life of the particular Church.'[6]

This principle is reflected in Art. 1 of the post-synodal statutes: 'The norms set out in these articles are provided to promote and foster the observance of the universal law of the Church; the general decrees of particular councils and of the Conference of Bishops and those canonical norms which the circumstances of diocesan life most require. These articles which form part of the *post-synodal declarations and decrees* are true juridic norms and together with other pre-existing local legislation, which has not been abrogated expressly, are binding. As prescribed in canon 8 § 2, they begin to oblige one month following their promulgation.' The manner of promulgation of local laws is determined by the legislator.[7] The post-synodal statutes or constitutions, expressed in articles, are the putting into concrete action the decisions of the diocesan bishop following the advice given to him by the people of God of the diocese in synod.

As a reflection of collegiality and fraternity, 'The diocesan Bishop is to communicate the text of the declarations and decrees of the synod to the Metropolitan [The Archbishop of Cashel and Emly] and to the Episcopal Conference.'[8]

Finally, 'When all matters concerning the synod shall have been completed, the diocesan Bishop will transmit, through the

---

6. *Instruction*, V, 2.
7. *The Code of Canon Law*, can. 8 § 2.
8. *The Code of Canon Law,* can. 467.

Pontifical Representative [the Apostolic Nuncio], a copy of the synodal documentation to the Congregation for Bishops or to the Congregation for the Evangelization of Peoples, for their information.'[9]

---

9. *Instruction,* V, 5.

Chapter Eight
Prayer on the Synod Journey
Betty Baker and Margaret O'Sullivan

The Synod is Launched

The Limerick Diocesan Synod was launched in St John's Cathedral with the celebration of Eucharist on Sunday, 7 December 2014. We, three hundred plus delegates, huddled in a school hall on a dark December Sunday trying to organise ourselves to move with lighted candles across the yard to the Church; at the bell toll to move, the sky opened. We arrived at the front door of the Church wet, cold, partners displaced and no light in our candles. We were glad to make landfall in a seat and shake off the beads of water from hair and brow! I hoped it wouldn't be symbolic of what lay ahead. The diocesan banner designed for the synod journey had as its inspirational statement: 'The Spirit of Truth will guide you.' Bishop Brendan Leahy unrolled a scroll and set us on a path of gathering, listening, discussing and praying across our parishes, families and diocese. The mandate we were sent forth with was to embrace the synod as an opportunity to create a Church that will fit the present day and to discern a vision to renew and heal, to welcome and include.

Wrapped in Prayer

> Then Moses summoned Joshua, and in the presence of all Israel, said to him, 'Be strong and courageous; you are going with this people into the land promised to our ancestors. You must lead them to possess this land as their heritage. The Living God will go before you, and will never fail you or desert you. So do not fear and never be disheartened.' (Deut 31:3)

This was one of the readings chosen for our prayer in the synod gathering. At the first gathering of the Preparatory Commission we were reminded that we were embarking on a courageous journey in the company of a God who would go before us and who would guide and lead us. On our part, we pledged to wrap the synod journey in prayer at all levels across the parishes and diocese. Each meeting began with prayer as we tried to attune our hearts to God whispering in the hearts of people. We were invited into the process of discernment, calling us to deep listening and reflective prayer leading to action.

Woven into the fabric of the synod journey, personal prayer and community prayer carried us through the two years of preparation. We were reminded often that all our deliberations were evolving under a canopy of faith, grounding our interactions in reflective and prayerful scaffolding.

A prayer card was designed and distributed to all parishes inviting the community to pray together for the synod each time the community gathered. This made its way onto kitchen tables, into classrooms, parish offices, halls, meeting rooms, hospitals and nursing homes and wherever people gathered to share and discuss the synod agenda.

Prayer on the Synod Journey

'Synod Sundays' were launched and special prayers, reflections and music were designed to focus hearts on the ongoing momentum of the synod. For those who could not actively be engaged in the day-to-day matters of the synod, prayer was our common link with each other on the ground and these moments kept us connected to the synod process. For some, the synod was still something of a 'mystery' at this stage.

Conscious of the strength of 'where two or three are gathered', pastoral areas assembled with their delegates and parishioners for communal prayer in the lead up to the synod. Scripture, reflection, music and ritual enriched and refreshed these gatherings. Delegates were sent out into the synod knowing the prayers of so many accompanied them.

Three Days

The opening Mass of the synod was celebrated on 3 April in St John's Cathedral. We were ready this time – even down to the weather! This modelled the best in liturgy, as collectively, we were energised by the gathered assembly, drawn in by symbol, colour and ritual, nourished by prayer, hymns and music and encircled by inclusion and a tangible sense of expectation. We prayed with sincere and expectant hope as our 'acceptable time' had come and we were on the threshold of this graced moment of synod. The introductory welcome, spoken in Irish, honoured the journey since the launch in 2014 and created a sense of gratitude and pride as we launched into our opening hymn, 'Rejoice, rejoice, let all the world believe, the Risen Lord now calls us to prosper in this place.' Our processional symbols of candles, scroll and flags spoke of light for the journey, commitment, community and belonging. The music of the Mass of St Ita, our Limerick patroness, was composed and shared across the diocese to be sung for this special occasion. The synod candle specially designed was blessed. At the conclusion of the

Mass, it lit our way as we followed its glow out of the Cathedral, holding the flame in our hearts until it would take its place in the assembly hall of the synod where it would continue to warm us and offer its burning light over the three days.

Prayer Moments

Our commitment to enfold the synod in prayer came to culmination during the days of synod. Thoughtful, creative, sacred spaces were central in the large gathering space. At set up, the synod floor was buzzing with technicians and a team of helpers. We were all fighting for our own little corners as we tried to find the best space possible to assemble our sacred space. Foliage and flowers and props littered the floor as we put up and pulled down in an effort to get it right. Our synod candle was lit each day as we gathered for inspiration around its generous, encouraging glow. A special booklet was provided to all delegates to enable maximum, active participation in the themed prayer movements of each day. Some of the synod themes were captured in the daily prayer rituals, especially that of journey, leadership, community and belonging, family, and going forth. The opening prayer of the synod was introduced with ritual and dance to the words of the hymn 'Gather': 'Gather from the east, gather from the west, gather from the highways too …' And what a moment of gathering it was as the music of harp and violin lifted our hearts to prepare us for this special beginning to our synod. We were deeply moved as we looked around the room and witnessed the sense of awe on people's faces and what felt like a blanket of goodness emanating from so many wonderful people at this moment of prayer. Our three days were flanked by prayer, our comings and goings were blessed and our faith connected us in ways we had not experienced as a community of close to four hundred participants.

Conclusion

Our closing Mass was again inclusive, rich in colour, ritual and symbol, music and song, enhanced once again by the beautiful surroundings of St John's Cathedral. The expectancy lingered on but was now tempered with an enormous sense of privilege and gratitude for being a part of this special time in our diocese. Our gospel for this Eucharist was the appearance of Jesus to the disciples by the sea of Tiberius. It resonated with us because, like the disciples, in our sending forth from this gathering we were charged with 'getting our nets ready', for the 'fishing' was only about to begin as we carried forward the message of the synod to the north and south, the east and west of our diocese and beyond. To ritualise the historic nature of our synod, a time capsule was prepared containing the scroll from the launch of the synod and the vision statements on each of the six themes. This will be held in the diocesan archives until it is opened by the bishop on Easter Sunday 2026.

Our final hymn was a fitting send-off as we sang:

> Good news in spoken word
> Joyfully our hearts have heard;
> O may the seed of God's love now grow,
> May we in fruitful deeds, gladly serve other's needs,
> That faith in action we may show.

As members of the Preparatory Commission with responsibility for liturgy, some of the high points included the opening Mass in the Cathedral and daily prayer in the synod hall. Having worked on the liturgy, which on paper looked organised and satisfactory, the sense of unity and celebration, life and energy I felt when all were gathered was beyond my expectations. The appreciation expressed by many for rich experiences of prayer and liturgy confirmed my own sense of the importance of preparation to participation. I sensed also a 'soulful' longing for creative rituals that touch and engage the deeper parts of ourselves. We tasted this in the synod days and hopefully an outcome of the synod will be the further exploration and development of this area.

Chapter Nine

Reflections along the Way: 'We Are where we Need to Be'

Éamonn Fitzgibbon

OVER THE YEARS, I HAVE WALKED MANY DIFFERENT stages of the Camino de Santiago de Compostela. I have sometimes walked with organised groups and at other times walked for weeks on my own. I have been on the busy Camino Frances or the very quiet Via de la Plata from the south. For this reason, I was very struck by the image of *camino* used by Bishop Brendan in his pastoral letter entitled 'Together in Mission: A Time to Begin Again'. Over the course of the synod I often thought how fitting the comparison is. When one walks the Camino, one can plan and study maps and guides but the way is still somewhat unknown and the path is only truly made by walking. Pilgrims on the Camino quickly learn that one needs to be able to let go of many things and truly travel light. One has to be willing to ask for direction. It is said of a diocesan synod that it is both a process and an event – in other words the journey and the destination – and I have learned that the journey is hugely important; patience and persistence is key. Again it is also said of a synod that while the meeting is important the gathering is even more so – in other words the agenda and the task of the three-day meeting is, of course, very significant but of equal (if not greater importance) is the gathering of people who are present at the meeting.

After I was asked by Bishop Brendan to coordinate the synod, I found myself regularly daunted by the task ahead – in fact when I thought of it all I could tend towards panic – but day by day we progressed along the way and I regularly consoled myself that we were 'where we need to be for now'. Most importantly, I learned that one cannot walk this way alone but only with others.

Along the way, I had to let go of many things – my expectations or plans, for example – and trust in God's Spirit and the wisdom of other wayfarers and wise guides.

The Delegates

As I reflect on the journey the most encouraging piece is the presence of so many delegates. Initially this was the biggest task – recruiting delegates from parishes and communities across the diocese who would truly reflect the diversity and richness of our diocesan community. Happily, we ended up with a tremendous group of delegates – over four hundred in all. Together we learned what it meant to be a delegate to a synod and walked the way towards April 2016. I was hugely heartened by the commitment and enthusiasm of our delegates.

I learned to trust the delegates, recognising that their wisdom is of the Spirit. This trust led to an entrusting whereby it was the delegates themselves who charted the course and determined the direction. They carried out the enormous task of listening to their communities – using a variety of methods to discern the hopes and fears, the joys and sorrows of the people with whom they live and work. It was then the delegates themselves who discerned and selected the themes that were brought forward to the synod.

Methodology
I have studied the theories and methodologies of theological reflection and the synod offered an opportunity to bring together in dialogue human experience, our tradition and cultural issues. The synod has been an opportunity to learn and listen, to reflect and wonder. The approach is inductive, affording due regard to the experience of people in their daily lives, listening to 'the joys and the hopes, the griefs and the anxieties of the people of this age' (GS, 1) and seeing there God's hand at work and hearing there the voice of the Spirit. Having listened to the concerns, hopes and joys of people through the listening process in 2015 the emerging issues were put into dialogue with the rich tradition through catechetical moments along the way.

Highlights
There have been a number of particular highlights. One moment along the way was figuring out how best to sort out or analyse all the data from the material that came in from the parishes and communities from the listening process. Approximately five thousand people expressed their views by means of questionnaires or at meetings or online. Indeed other creative methods were used, including Facebook, informal listening methods and others. We were faced with a vast amount of material presented in a number of different formats. An even greater challenge was to be true to a discernment method. To complete this task, we assembled fifteen people who would help and they in turn attended a 'fishbowl' type training in which they 'eavesdropped' on six 'experts' from different disciplines. It was truly fascinating to hear how others would undertake the task and we were able to draw on the different expertise to come up with solid guidelines to ensure consistency across all fifteen 'coders'. I won't pretend the actual task of going through the material was terribly exciting in itself but it was an honour

and humbling to be in a position to read through and listen to the voice of the people. It is also a source of pride that we can honestly say that, in spite of the vast amount of material, we read through and took account of each and every contribution.

It has also been a unique privilege for me, as the one who had responsibility for coordinating the various aspects of the synod, to have had direct and personal contact with some wonderful and truly inspiring people. I had read and studied the theological writings of the Dominican theologian Fr Paul Philibert and now I was in a position to invite him to Ireland and during his stay to spend time in his company. Similarly, in the course of the preparation for the synod I had the privilege of meeting Níall McLaughlin, the renowned architect, and, of course, Sir Harry Burns, the former chief medical officer for Scotland. When I say this was a perk of the job I mean so sincerely. Of course, there was also the interaction with many people locally, who have acted as wise guides to us on our journey.

Conclusion

I had the opportunity over the course of the synod to travel throughout the diocese and meet groups of delegates. I am struck by the truly transformative effect that being on this journey together has had on all of us. When occasionally I found myself looking too far ahead and feeling overwhelmed, I would remind myself (as one does on the Camino), 'We are where we need to be.'

CHAPTER TEN

Catechesis and the Synod

Lorraine Buckley

CATECHESIS PLAYED AN ESSENTIAL PART OF OUR SYNOD journey and continues to be a necessary strand of the implementation of our pastoral plan. The *General Directory for Catechesis* describes catechesis as 'nothing other than the process of transmitting the gospel, as the Christian community has received it, understands it, celebrates it, lives it and communicates it in many ways'.[1] Catechesis, then, involves handing on what we have received, understanding it in the light of scripture and tradition, celebrating it in our liturgy and prayer and putting it into practice by living the gospel in our daily lives. In a very real sense the whole synod was a catechetical experience as it was a formative journey in which we, the Christian community in Limerick, engaged with the gospel in all these aspects. Our synodal process also had specific moments of catechesis in which we were invited to engage with a particular aspect of the gospel as individuals or in groups.

The Church does not canonise any particular method of catechesis, but invites us to use with liberty 'everything that is

---

1. *General Directory for Catechesis*, 105.

true, everything that is noble, everything that is good and pure, everything that we love and honour and everything that can be thought virtuous or worthy of praise' (Phil 4:8). The synod employed a variety of different means for creating catechetical moments: talks and workshops on a variety of themes (on the synod itself, the nature and mission of the Church, the Church and culture, the relationship between sports and religion, Limerick and its people, etc.), booklets, diocesan newspaper inserts, videos on how to read scripture using the *Lectio Divina* method, radio interviews and letters to be read by delegates at Mass. The synod website (www.synod2016.com) was also to be a useful means of giving those not directly involved as delegates the opportunity for engaging with the talks, videos, resources and notes online. It is impossible to do justice to the breadth and depth of the catechesis offered during the synod in such a short article, but two themes in particular were constant: (1) the role of the Holy Spirit; and (2) the priesthood of the faithful.

One of the first questions Bishop Leahy invited us to reflect upon was 'Who leads the Church?' In a series of commentaries on the Acts of the Apostles, Bishop Leahy encouraged us to notice the Holy Spirit at work in our lives and in our synod journey.[2] Listening to the voice of the Holy Spirit in the voices of those who responded to the listening process, in the voices of the delegates, in the voices of the observers, and especially in the voices of those who spoke for the marginalised, was a constant thread running throughout the synod preparations and the three-day event.

Father Paul Philibert's talk 'What Will the Synod Mean for You?' also touched on this theme at the inaugural meeting of

---

2. See Brendan Leahy, *Who Leads the Church? Noticing the Holy Spirit at Work – Extracts from The Acts of the Apostles with Commentaries by Bishop Brendan Leahy*, Dublin: Veritas, 2015.

delegates. Father Philibert reminded us that 'the Holy Spirit is the great iconographer who, using our bodies, our community, our actions, and our attitudes, creates an image of God's people portraying the kingdom of God'. It was to the Holy Spirit that we were to turn again and again while we discerned the way forward, leading Bishop Leahy to remark that the synod was an event of the Holy Spirit. Father Philibert unpacked the themes of the Church as communion, the People of God, the Body of Christ and asked of us: 'Can the Diocese of Limerick, its parishes, and its people, become a clear and persuasive sacrament of the presence of the risen Lord?'

The answer to that question is a decisive yes by virtue of our baptism. This was the second key theme of our catechesis. Donal Harrington wrote two catechetical sessions in which he invited us to reflect on baptism and Eucharist. First, Donal invited reflection upon what it means to be baptised, to participate in the one priesthood of Christ as priest (gift), prophet (presence) and king (leader). We are all (lay, clerics and religious) called to be a gift to each other, to make Christ present in our families and communities, to lead through service, recognising, encouraging and supporting the talents of others, in order to make God's kingdom more and more of a reality on earth. Leadership in the Church, then, is not left to a few; Donal speaks instead of 'every member ministry' or to use a sporting term 'leaders all over the field'. Secondly, Donal invited us to reflect on the relationship between community and the Eucharist, posing the questions: 'How can we build community in our liturgy, in the breaking of bread?' and 'How can we build community in life, in the washing of feet?' In other words, as the Body of Christ, how can we act eucharistically every day?

It was in this context that the three-day synod event took place – looking at how the Church in Limerick could incarnate the gospel anew. As Bishop Leahy reminded us, the Word of God is 'alive and active' (Heb 4:12) and wants to 'bring a revolution in our thoughts, our affections and our will. It helps us see things differently, judge situations with a gospel logic and act as new men and women. As St Augustine says, a new person sings a new song.'[3] That is now our challenge: to allow the gospel to transform us so that we can sing a new song of hope as we look to implement the diocesan pastoral plan, 'Moving Forward Together in Hope'.

---

3. Leahy, *Who Leads the Church?*, p. 8.

CHAPTER ELEVEN
Communicating the Synod
Noirín Lynch

'Communication has the power to build bridges, to enable encounter and inclusion, and thus to enrich society.' (Pope Francis, World Communication Day, 2016)[1]

COMMUNICATION IS BOTH AN IMPARTING OF information and a means of connection. In a world drowning in instant information and coming to terms with 'media bubbles', we can no longer assume that the news we send out is seen, let alone that it is read, considered and responded to. Thus, the way we engage in communication is as important as the information shared.

I believe that good communication for a Catholic diocese is a pastoral task, not simply an administrative one, and is always

---

1. Pope Francis, 'Message of his Holiness Pope Francis for the 50th World Communications Day', https://w2.vatican.va/content/francesco/en/messages/communications/documents/papa-francesco_20160124_messaggio-comunicazioni-sociali.html, accessed 24 November 2016.

an exercise in co-responsibility – we share news so as to include the wider community. Each event or invitation is part of a wider vision, and communication is the vehicle that enables very diverse communities across this diocese to notice that their seemingly separate strands are part of one coherent message.

There was a broad team involved in communication for our synod. Some were involved across the process – such as Chris Culhane, our website developer – and others joined as needed – such as Eugene Hogan, who managed all media relations, and myself, Noirín Lynch, with responsibility for social media. As always, the administrator, Karen Kiely, took care of internal communication with grace and ease.

Moments of Communication on our Synod

The diocesan synod was a seminal event in our diocese and over a number of years it gathered a large group that was representative of all aspects of our community of communities. Across about three years, pastoral communication took account of moments like these:

- Launch: Launching the synod and inviting faith communities to nominate delegates.
- Internal: Communication with the delegates across the core eighteen-month process.
- Diocesan: Updating the wider parishes, schools and faith communities.
- The synod event, April 2016.
- Post-synod: Sharing the good news and communicating legacy issues.

Methods of Communication in our Synod

The ultimate method of communication is, of course, person to person. In many cases, delegates who were inspired by the experience found themselves telling friends and family – like

Mary Magdalene saying, 'I have seen the Lord' (Jn 20:18). However, our synod communications also included the following:

- A website (www.synod2016.com), which has served as a source of news for those interested, a library of resources for delegates and an archive for the synod process.
- Ongoing contact with local newspapers and radio.
- 'The Synod Script' – three special supplements in local papers.[2]
- Social media – particularly during the synod event itself.
- 'Synod Sundays' in parishes where delegates updated parishioners at Sunday Mass.

Social Media and the Synod

A friend approached me on day two of the synod and thanked me for the social media work. I demurred politely but she insisted on its importance. 'I am here as a delegate,' she said. 'My husband – a member of a parish council – is at home with the children. Yesterday he followed the synod all day, he knew what to pray for and could see the joy. We were able to speak about it at home last night and both feel part of this together. This is important work.'

We already have a diocesan Facebook page, but decided to create both Facebook and Twitter accounts for Synod2016. While they were active across the whole process, they really came into their own over the week of the synod. Their purpose was to offer the wider diocese live access to a seminal moment in the diocese – through reports, photo/video and prayer requests.

---

2. The day after the synod, a full-colour comprehensive sixteen-page 'The Synod Script' was published. Seventy-five thousand copies were sent out through local papers and parishes, and were snapped up immediately.

Social Media in the Weeks before the Synod

The Synod2016 Facebook page reported local preparation and all synod gatherings in advance of the synod. This mostly reached only a small group but served as a reminder to delegates or added to the informal network of prayer partners abroad.

In the ten days before the synod we stepped up posts considerably to create awareness and widen that group. A series of short Facebook videos of local leaders sending best wishes to the upcoming synod proved popular.[3]

Social Media at the Synod

I worked with Chris Culhane, who manages the synod website, to get all the social media information up on the website in real time. Dropbox was very helpful in sharing the large number of videos and photos quickly. At the same time, Eugene Hogan was working with a team to develop broader content for 'The Synod Script', a detailed account of outcomes, which was published in local papers the following week. The two approaches were complementary and ensured the widest possible audience were aware, informed and enthused.

Daily Facebook posts began at 7 a.m. Scheduled posts informed those at home where we were in the process and asked for prayers. Photos and videos of people were added across the day, usually one after each tea break. Each evening saw a spike in interest as delegates went home! Many said they loved showing the pictures to family and the discussions it created.

We estimate that between fifteen thousand and twenty

---

3. Videos included Na Piarsaigh GAA (local All-Ireland champions), the Mayor of Limerick city, Moyross students on the Camino, our Papal Nuncio and other Church leaders. These were shown twice daily for the week beforehand and each had between one thousand and four thousand views.

thousand people engaged with us on social media that weekend. Up to two hundred people at a time were logged on to the website across the three days. There was a very high degree of participation on posts at all times. To make things manageable, all Facebook posts were automatically retweeted, and Twitter had a small but dedicated following.

Chapter Twelve
Facilitating the Synod Process
Martin Kennedy

IN ESTABLISHING THIS SYNODAL PROCESS, BISHOP Leahy was looking for concrete implementable conclusions in a missionary key that would address the pastoral challenges of the diocese at this time. And while Canon Law stipulates that the synod authority rests solely with the bishop – from his approval and promulgation of the synod decrees – effectively Brendan Leahy was inviting some four hundred delegates to engage with him in a decision-making process. This fundamentally shaped the facilitation task. How could a group of four hundred people of diverse backgrounds and experience, in communion with their bishop, engage with the pastoral issues facing the diocese and come to informed, prayerful and realistic conclusions? How could they do that in a way that avoided a narrowly 'political' approach based around already given positions and commitments? Would it be possible to have a process that was genuinely a listening one open to the promptings of the Spirit?

A factor apparent from the outset gave grounds for hope on these questions. This might broadly be described as the 'good humour' of the delegates. People were glad to be involved, were looking for a process that respected their contribution and were disposed to respecting such a process in turn. The challenge then was to design a way of engaging the delegates throughout the synod process, one that recognised and tapped into their energy and insight, one that was genuinely participative. Broadly speaking we managed this. The delegates stayed on board – they held their good humour, participated well and came to a set of concrete conclusions. While there was debate and difference, at no point did the process collapse into rancour and division.

I'll try to describe here some of the main elements in the process that facilitated this positive outcome. For me, the central one was that the process was a practical one – the delegates engaged in a set of concrete tasks rather than a more general discussion about 'issues'. They were supported in those tasks by a range of inputs, but always with a view to a hands-on application. In that way, the journey of the synod could be described as an 'apprenticeship' in discernment and decision-making, and I think that fundamentally suited the people.

The journey followed a standard three-step process: SEE–JUDGE–ACT. At each step there was a job to be done.

- SEE underscored the basic missionary impetus of the synod. It involved listening to the lives of the people of the diocese. Delegates from the parishes and from the range of educational and social ministries were asked to organise listening events with the groups they were ministering to.
- The second stage – JUDGE – was about the delegates engaging in a prayerful discernment on the results of the listening, with a view to coming to a decision on what issues the synod would focus on.
- The third stage – ACT – involved the delegates developing concrete proposals for actions to address these issues – proposals that would be brought to the synod to be discussed and voted on.

The detailed planning and facilitation of the synod occurred within this overall framework.

See: Paying Attention to the Reality of Life in Limerick

In chapter five, Rosemary O'Connor details the variety of listening methods that were made available to the delegates and the training sessions offered for these in early 2015. The delegates went about their task, engaged with some five thousand people and completed their listening actions by the summer. This stage of the process was completed by two further actions. In June, a morning gathering of delegates was held to 'check in' on how they found the listening experience and to outline the next steps. A basic pattern for full delegate gatherings was established here that broadly held for all subsequent gatherings – prayer, short inputs, small-group discussion and open forum.

Delegates were assigned to mixed, small groups of no more than eight. Each group had a designated facilitator drawn from delegates with known facilitation experience. The facilitators were provided with a template for the discussions, outlining steps and timings, and were briefed on that template during the registration and coffee hour at the start of the day. A simple template for recording strongly felt points in the discussions was also provided and the facilitators were asked to identify somebody from their small group to manage that.

This structure had a number of advantages. It meant that we were able to keep to time, and some forty to fifty small groups could operate simultaneously more or less at the same pace. It also significantly impacted on the open forum. The open forum was always going to be a challenge. How do you provide a space for people to speak their voice in a group that size and in a limited time? If everybody spoke for just one minute on any one topic, it would take over six hours. However, the delegates were very clued in to that issue, and the last thing they wanted was to be subjected to individual grandstanding and endless talking. So they accepted and worked within proposed open-forum ground rules.

- Contributions should articulate briefly one point felt strongly in the small group.
- If a point has already been made it doesn't need to be repeated.
- Nobody should speak twice until everybody that wanted to had spoken once.

This meant that the open forum wasn't a reporting back on small-group discussions. It was a platform for strongly felt concerns. In that setting it was possible to check back on what was most strongly and widely felt. The collective body language of the assembly (applause, murmurings, etc.) could be read and a question put back – Are we hearing you right? You are happy with this? You have concerns about that? The fact that each small-group discussion had a written record on strong points raised was also a help. People felt assured that individual points made in small groups, whether articulated at the open forum or not, would receive attention.

- The second action to close this listening phase involved the establishment of a working group to study and summarise the results of the listening exercises. This was a substantial and difficult task given the huge volume of material gathered. The key task of the group was to be of service to the delegates in presenting back to them in digestible form the main patterns arising from the listening.

Judge: Discerning the Results of the Listening Exercise to Determine the Synod Agenda

An assembly of the delegates was held in October 2015 to present the results of the listening and identify the key themes to be addressed at the synod in April 2016. This involved two key elements. Firstly, a presentation from the working group on the listening survey patterns clustered under twelve headings. This was done in a very comprehensive, detailed and even technical manner. While there were some fears that the presentation might be experienced by delegates as too technical and complicated, in fact it was very positively received. What delegates appreciated most was the obvious level of attention given to their listening work from the previous spring. There was a strong sense that the listening had been honoured and the voice of the people of Limerick gathered in a clear manner.

The second element was the actual discernment and decision on what topics would be addressed at the synod. Delegates were asked to prioritise six themes from what was presented by the working group. (We settled on six on the basis of what we felt could reasonably be managed over the course of a three-day synod.) This was a practical exercise in prayerful decision-making by the delegates in anticipation of the actual synod itself. Jessie Rogers designed the discernment process and details it in chapter six. Her process provided an opportunity for the delegates to be coached in discernment with a very practical, hands-on and immediate opportunity for application. The facilitation of the day was organised on that basis. As can be seen from Jessie's piece, the prayer and action were blended into a single movement – the prayer was an action and the action a prayer. For me, this was one of the highlights of the whole process.

Act: Developing and Voting on Action Proposals
Once the October discernment was completed on the broad synod agenda, the next objective was to have prepared a set of action proposals, published and circulated to all delegates in advance of the synod proper in April. As noted above, this was

to be led by the delegates themselves. This work was done in two stages. Firstly, as detailed in chapter eleven, a series of pre-Christmas gatherings under the title 'People of God: People of Limerick' was organised to address in a general way the synod themes. Speakers with backgrounds in theology and sociology offered inputs to the delegates both on Church teachings and traditions in relation to the six themes, and on the reality of life in Limerick, again in relation to the themes. The purpose here was to seek to strike a balance between the values of a broad Church and society vision and a commitment to local and particular needs.

Following this series, delegates were invited into a process for the development of concrete proposals. Two workshops were run for each of the six themes. Delegates could go to whichever workshops and themes they had particular energy for. The method used at the workshops was 'open space'. People named ideas they had for possible actions. These ideas were postered and placed around the walls of the meeting room. Everybody then did a 'gallery walk', studying the posters and placing a sticker on the ones they felt were especially important. People then opted for whichever poster they had most energy for. Whoever gathered around the poster became the planning group with a brief to develop the action idea into a concrete proposal following a standard template. The groups either finished their task over the two workshops or arranged to finalise it soon after. Support was offered to groups as needed.

The action proposals were submitted and published in the synod workbook. Some editing was done to deal with overlaps and duplications, resulting in some one hundred specific proposals for voting at the synod. This part of the process was a bit frenetic – the synod deadline was approaching fast and pressure was on the planning groups to get their proposals in. It might have been better had more time been available. Also it is understandable that having gone through the detailed work of preparing their particular proposal not all delegates were happy with the editing done, and the grouping of some proposals. However, no substantive proposal was left out. The synod workbook was published and circulated a week before the synod itself. Along with the proposals grouped and subgrouped under the six headings, there was also background material and a process for praying with the proposals in advance of the synod.

The final part of the action step was the voting at the synod itself, which met for three days in April.

The first two days covered the action proposals on the six themes. Managing the time available to process one hundred votes in a prayerful, calm and participative manner was a challenge. The availability of electronic voting equipment was a great help. We used the same process for each of the six sets of proposals covering six two-hour sessions on the Friday and Saturday. A short presentation was made covering the impact that the proposals sought to achieve, the rationale behind that and where they emerged from in the original listening. The Bishop spoke to each set, sharing his perspective. Given the synodality of the gathering – the partnership of bishop and people together – it was important for both parties to hear from each other and to take into account each other's views. This was followed by small-group discussion along the same lines as above, and then open forum. We felt it was really important to have an effective open forum where people would have the chance to express any strongly felt concerns on the actions before the vote. In order to manage the time available, we agreed to a register system for the open forum. If somebody wanted to speak on a given topic, they simply registered their interest. We asked people to confine their contribution to one minute and to speak only once. All those who registered to speak were called first. People were hugely respectful of this process and the open forums were very calm and powerful spaces where a range of views were expressed and listened to. After the open forum we moved on to the vote. As in October, the vote itself was an act of prayer, again facilitated by Jessie. The electronic voting system enabled instant visual feedback on each vote, and even though we had one hundred voting calls, it didn't feel heavy or drawn out and we finished each of the sessions within the allocated time.

The Sunday morning session dealt with the extra-synodal matters. The open forum at that session was, for me, one of the most graced moments in any Church gathering I have ever attended. We followed the same process of registering and keeping the inputs short. The quality of the sharing and the listening was very powerful. If ever there was a reason not to be afraid of a national synod it was this. People of very different viewpoints showed that they had the grace and capacity to be both truthful to themselves and respectful of one another.

CHAPTER THIRTEEN
Accompanying and Administering the Synod
Karen Kiely

WHEN BISHOP BRENDAN CONVOKED A SYNOD HE ALSO put the necessary infrastructure in place resourcing the work with a synod office, support staff and a budget. I was already working with the Diocese of Limerick, having previously worked as administrator of the Diocesan Pastoral Centre, and I was then working in the finance office of the diocese. I was now seconded to work as administrator of the diocesan synod.

A key aspect of this role was communicating with and supporting the delegates to the synod. As delegates were recruited I filed their application forms and once they were nominated I created a database that enabled me to reach out to them by phone, letter, email and text in the subsequent months. The importance of this cannot be overstated; delegates attended many meetings and fulfilled a variety of roles, and having a central point of contact where they could voice concerns, ask questions or seek reassurance was vital. Simultaneously, we were able to communicate the details of events quickly and easily. This was more than an administrative task – it was also an act of accompaniment and over time I was able to build a relationship with the delegates whereby they felt comfortable contacting me with any concerns or queries.

Throughout the process, communication in a planned and developmental fashion was essential – to say again and again what it was we were doing, what our hopes and plans for the synod were and to outline the upcoming stages of the journey.

A synod logo and tag line helped to create identity. Use of parish newsletters, 'Synod Sundays' in the parishes, bulletin inserts, video presentations and radio spots enabled us to communicate the message.

Another aspect of my accompaniment and administrative role was attendance at many meetings and recording the minutes. This was particularly important at meetings of the Preparatory Commission, as this was where each aspect of the synod journey was carefully discussed and planned.

During the synod journey, we held over twenty-three meetings (some plenary, some regional) with delegates. Alongside these there were also times of catechesis for delegates to enable them to deepen their own understanding of the issues that had been identified through the listening process. Catechesis and formation on the issues which emerged ensured that the discussion at the synod itself was informed. We organised public lecture series, clergy meetings and training events. Each of these required significant administrative support, what might be called the three Rs – registering, recording, resourcing.

Early in the process, we committed to ensuring that our delegates and others would be well treated, venues would be warm and welcoming; hospitality and generosity were to be clearly evident. We decided to use hotel venues and delegates – who were voluntarily giving their spare time – would at least be guaranteed good lunches on full training days, and have comfortable seating, along with sufficient tea/coffee breaks.

I have no doubt that our commitment to the welfare of delegates was instrumental in ensuring that so many delegates stayed with the process. I came to know many hotels and hotel staff and we also had some interesting choices of venue, perhaps the most popular being the conference facilities at Thomond Park.

We hosted sessions on topics such as the identity and mission of the city, sport, architecture, culture, history, young people and social issues.

An essential administrative task was liaising with Chris Culhane, who managed the synod website. The website came to be populated with accounts of each step of the journey – reports, texts, photographs and video clips.

The event itself in April 2016 was, of course, a major administrative task. We chose Mary Immaculate College as the venue. The pre-synod event in the College on 12 March, which served as a dress rehearsal, was a great help. This dry run enabled us to identify any snags or difficulties that might arise at the synod itself. By now, the staff engaged with the synod had grown significantly as teams of people gathered around each aspect of the event – communication, security, catering, hosting, meeting rooms. Every detail had to be planned. We even nominated a timekeeper complete with bell to marshal each part of the synod days. People were assigned groups and a badge that served as a code for them and us, indicating where they should be at each moment.

Finally, another very important aspect of my role as administrator of the synod was my work with Éamonn Fitzgibbon, the Synod Director – mostly reassuring him that all would be well, that 'we are where we need to be now' and not to panic.

CHAPTER FOURTEEN
Back to the Future: Synod 2016
David Bracken

POPE FRANCIS, SPEAKING AT A GATHERING OF THE Italian Church in Florence in 2015, remarked, 'We are not living an era of change but a change of era.' 'The reform of the church,' he continued, involves 'grafting yourself to and rooting yourself in Christ, leaving yourself to be guided by the Spirit.' The recent synod in Limerick challenged the current tired narrative of retrenchment and decline in the Irish Church. Notwithstanding the enormous challenges facing the Catholic community, participants were left with the hope that, rooted in Christ and guided by the Spirit, to reprise the words of Francis, 'all will be possible with genius and creativity'.

The walls of the synod hall in Mary Immaculate College that welcomed the four hundred or so delegates were lined with images that illustrated the rich patrimony of the Diocese of Limerick, its people, parishes and churches. Much of that heritage dates from the late nineteenth century and the ecclesial certainties of that period find physical expression in the church buildings that dominate the Limerick landscape; the product of a great Catholic building boom that characterised those years.

The spire of St John's Cathedral (1882) in the heart of the city is visible from all approaches. The churches of Saints Peter and Paul, Kilmallock (1889), Saint Mary's, Rathkeale (1873) and Our Lady of the Immaculate Conception, Ballingarry (1879), to name but a few, speak of a community that has arrived; as does the wonderful complex of buildings in Kilfinane, St Andrew's Church (1884), turreted presbytery and convent. However, the humble simplicity of the eighteenth-century Church of St John, Cratloe (commenced 1791) is more in keeping with the sensibilities and anxieties of the present age. Indeed, it is perhaps helpful to look to the Irish Church in the late eighteenth century as we seek a pathway in the twenty-first.

The eighteenth-century Church was beginning to emerge from centuries of obscurity, although its future was far from certain as illustrated by the loss of the Irish continental colleges occasioned by the French Revolution. In 1786 the then bishop of Limerick, Dr Denis Conway (1722–96), submitted a *relatio status* report to Rome detailing the state of the diocese. Forty parishes, five of them in the city, served a Catholic population of about seventy thousand people. The number of priests is not stated but a report by his successor, Dr John Young (1746–1813), in 1802 noted that fifty-eight priests ministered in the diocese, including ten regulars, Augustinians, Dominicans and Franciscans who served for the most part within the confines of the city.

While they were sufficient in number, Conway expressed fears of a future scarcity of priests as many newly ordained clergy eschewed the Irish mission for the relative comfort of France where they were educated. There was no convent of nuns in the diocese, no clerical seminary and no confraternities in the parishes. A programme of reform initiated by Conway included regular parish visitation, the establishment of a confraternity of the Blessed Sacrament in every parish and continuous formation for diocesan clergy. Indeed, St Munchin's College was founded in 1795 to provide for the education of priests. The impetus for renewal is also evident in the establishment of a religious community under the direction of Bishop Conway in St John's in October 1786; the statutes and rules of the congregation were printed in Limerick in 1790.

Reforms continued under Dr Young, who succeeded as bishop in 1796 with the notable formation of a catechetical society. In December 1801, the Society of the Christian Doctrine had thirty-nine catechists, twenty-eight men and eleven women who provided catechesis to hundreds of children across the diocese. The nascent renewal of religious life alluded to above is reflected in a letter to Bishop Young written in *c.*1796 from the Society of St Joseph whose members included many young people, 'remarkable for their zeal and piety'. The letter refers to their intention of leading the single life and requests approval of their rule.

In remarks that recall the experience of the late eighteenth-century Church sketched above, Fr Joseph Ratzinger, the future Pope Benedict, predicted in 1969 that the Church of tomorrow 'will become small and will have to start afresh more or less from the beginning'. He further observed that it 'will no longer be able to inhabit many of the edifices she built in prosperity'. As this new reality dawns, we recognise that much of what has served us well in the past no longer meets our need. At the outset, Fr Paul Philibert suggested that the synod represented a unique opportunity to refound the Diocese of Limerick. That we might begin again with courage – as those who went before us have done countless times – to write a new chapter for a new era in the millennial history of our diocese.

PART THREE: DESTINATION

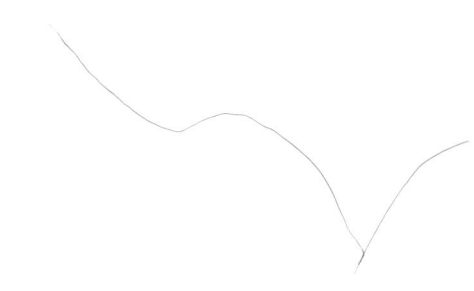

CHAPTER FIFTEEN
The Synod Event
Karen Kiely

IT IS SAID OF A SYNOD THAT WHILE THE BUSINESS OF the meeting is important, the gathering is even more so. In other words, the agenda and the task of the three-day meeting is, of course, very significant but of equal (if not greater) importance is the gathering of people who are present at the meeting.

On the agenda were over one hundred proposals to create a more unified, inclusive and accessible Church in the Diocese of Limerick and these were voted on over the first two days of the three-day synod. Some ninety-seven proposals were approved across six themes covering a wide range of issues, from dealing with hurt in the Church to enhancing its faith formation, hospitality and welcome.

In addition to the proposals for positive change to the Church, a range of 'universal issues' beyond the jurisdiction of the diocese were also discussed at the synod on the third day.

Even though electronic voting was rejected in the political world we found it extremely useful at the synod. Voting was carried out by means of zappers resembling old-fashioned TV remotes. These devices allowed each person to vote one of three ways: by pressing the number 1 to say, 'Yes, I strongly support this proposal and consider it a priority'; by pressing 2 to say, 'Yes, I support this proposal'; or by pressing 3 to say, 'No, I do not support this proposal'. This system enabled us to vote quickly and efficiently across 101 proposals. The proposals were grouped around six topics (Community and Sense of Belonging; Family; Transmission of Faith; New Models of Leadership; Liturgy and Life; Young People). After a broad introduction to each topic, the Bishop offered a short commentary on his overview of the proposals in that topic. There was time for a facilitated group discussion (again in an atmosphere of discernment), a brief time for plenary discussion (one minute maximum per speaker), further discussion and then the vote. Results appeared immediately on the large screen and so we were also able to immediately get an initial read on the result by displaying the percentages of those who voted for each of the three options.

Among the topics that emerged as key issues was 'lifelong faith formation' – initiatives for children, young adults, parents and adults – to ensure that people were equipped to deliver the good news of the gospel at all stages of their lives.

Lay leadership is also a key issue and the development of lay ecclesial ministries with an equal role for women was firmly endorsed. Alongside this was support for priests; that there would be 'team ministry'. The idea that it won't be possible for priests to continue forever as lone rangers for the parish and that the parish would have to work together in cluster formations came across strongly. Another key issue was safeguarding and this is no surprise, given its importance.

The gathering of people is of equal and perhaps greater importance than the agenda. Many delegates spoke of what a powerful experience it was for them simply to be with other delegates and diocesan clergy in such a participative and reflective setting. Indeed, one of the high points of the synod was a spontaneous standing ovation in support and appreciation of their ministry offered to priests. The facilitator was Martin Kennedy, who was excellent. Jessie Rogers (lecturer in sacred scripture, St Patrick's College, Maynooth) accompanied him. Jessie's role was greatly appreciated. At the beginning of and during each session, she led the synod gathering in moving into a mode of discerning what the Spirit wanted of us. A feature of the synod that many found moving was the range of brief greetings from representatives of other churches, ecclesial communities and faith communities.

Many non-delegates, who simply attended, enriched the opening and closing liturgies in the Cathedral with enthusiastic participation, many thousands followed the updates on the website (synod2016.com), and our small newspaper, 'The Synod Script', which went into the local newspapers and was distributed at Sunday Masses, was enthusiastically received throughout the diocese.

Chapter Sixteen
Synod Moments of Grace Sustaining Us on a Journey
Éamonn Fitzgibbon

THE PHRASE WE CHOSE FOR OUR SYNOD WAS 'Journeying Together in Faith'. Words and mottos are all very well – they connect and make sense at a head level – but over the three days of the synod, I had particular experiences where these words rang true at the level of heart and soul. My phone was busy during the days leading up to the synod as a variety of messages came in by text or email. Many texted to send best wishes and convey prayer messages; a small number of our delegates were unable to be present because of illness, a number were in the middle of cancer treatment; others sent apologies because of bereavement. As these various messages came I realised that over the previous two years the four hundred delegates to the synod had truly become a community. As we journeyed together, friendships had been formed and a unity and mutual concern had grown within the group. This found expression in the synod through the way in which various opinions, differing viewpoints and disparate positions could be named openly and without fear. Voices were heard respectfully and the truth was, indeed, spoken in love – *veritas in caritate*.

I had a number of particular 'grace moments' each day when I recognised God's Spirit present in a powerful way. On Friday, a woman spoke very movingly about the experience of bereavement and the need for compassion and love towards those who are in grief. This intervention set a tone whereby delegates could speak from the heart.

On Saturday, as part of our Interfaith Observers Group, we were joined in the afternoon by Imam Shaykh Dr Umar Al-Qadri and Eva Coombs from the Jewish community. Jessie Rogers, who was our facilitator on discernment, led us in a beautiful prayer about the call of Abraham. Jessie had not realised that at that moment we would have representatives of the three Abrahamic faiths – the three faiths who have Abraham as our 'father in faith' – and, in fact, she had prepared that prayer earlier in the week. Some might call this a happy coincidence; I recognise it for what it is – the Holy Spirit reminding us that a synod is, indeed, a Spirit-led event.

On Sunday afternoon, during an Open Forum on the Universal Church issues and in the midst of a lively debate in which many strongly held and deeply felt views were aired, I noticed many priests seemed a little uncomfortable and vulnerable. It is true to say that sometimes negative comment on Church can be taken personally by us priests as we can become so identified with our role. Anyway, out of nowhere a lay delegate said she wanted to acknowledge the good work done by priests and religious. Spontaneously, all the lay people in the room rose to their feet for sustained applause. It was an emotional and uplifting moment for the priests who were present.

Once more the Spirit was reminding us that God is walking with us, accompanying us as we 'journey together in faith'. It is these grace moments on the journey of synod – and on the journey of life – that sustain us along the way.

Chapter Seventeen
Synod Puts Building Blocks in Place for the Future: A Priest's Perspective
Tony Mullins

IT IS FAIR TO SAY THAT WHEN BISHOP BRENDAN convoked a synod in September 2014, few of us could have foreseen just how inclusive it would be. The Church had come through its most turbulent period of the modern era, perhaps ever, and a period of introspection was more than timely. But if there was any doubt as to just how deep the Church in Limerick would be willing to look, the answer became quickly apparent.

In short, this was a historic eighteen-month journey along which we had the most forensic examination of the Church imaginable. Under Fr Éamonn Fitzgibbon's direction, every issue was probed, no question left unasked. Concerns were addressed with incredible honesty. We learned from the bad, brought the good with us and earnestly planned for the future so that our Church in Limerick could move on, laity and clergy side by side, with purpose and vigour.

It all crystallised in April 2016 when over one hundred proposals across six themes were considered and voted on, putting in place building blocks for a new era for the Church in Limerick. Each and every proposal had its own merits, though each of us as delegates had our own particular preferences. One of the most important proposals for me was that we must reach out to those who feel excluded from the Church, because of the attitudes and teachings of the Church and those whose trust has been betrayed. We must do whatever is necessary to rebuild trust and attempt to heal the hurts and stay trying until we do.

I was pleased to see that the synod delegates acknowledged the dedicated work of teachers and chaplains in the evangelisation of children and young people in our Catholic schools, both primary and secondary. Strengthening the links between home, school and parish is also a hugely important issue for me. Bridging the disconnect will strengthen family, community and Church.

Another aspect of the synod that heartened me greatly and strengthened the sense of inclusiveness, not just for the synod itself but also for the future, was the presence of other Church leaders and the other faith communities. I found that incredibly affirming and moving. Their genuine messages of goodwill and prayer were deeply uplifting and we look forward to deepening relationships ahead. There was a very strong acknowledgement that there are a lot of positives to build on. In the diocese, we already have support services for families and individuals provided by the Limerick Social Service Centre, Henry Street, which is an agency of the diocese set up by the late Bishop Henry Murphy. There is the work of the Diocesan Youth Ministry Team operating from the Diocesan Pastoral Centre under the leadership of Fr Chris O'Donnell and Aoife Walsh. These diocesan services provide us with very strong foundations upon which we can hope to build, ensuring that many of the initiatives envisaged by the delegates at the synod will become a reality. We are blessed to have in our diocese the resources of Mary Immaculate College, the venue for the synod, and the wisdom and ministry of so many religious congregations.

Synod Puts Building Blocks in Place for the Future

The proposal for appointing lay administrators to pastoral areas is another really positive development and will take the burden off priests and allow them to concentrate on sacramental life. The synod delegates also agreed that priests will work more closely together in Pastoral Area Teams and this will become the norm into the future.

For a lot of delegates, the final motion of the synod, on establishing a working group to explore where women can play a leadership role in the governance of the Church, was a high point. It was an absolute affirmation of the role of women in the Church and was a necessary acknowledgement of the contribution they are making.

Working with so many people throughout this process was a privilege and that's a privilege that has begun at home in my own parish, Dromin-Athlacca. My fellow delegates from this parish have been so enthusiastic, so committed to the process, and that, too, has been enriching.

And now we continue this journey. This is the beginning of something new, something great. No doubt there are going to be challenges along the way but I cannot see anything except this bearing fruit. We have a huge bank of positivity built up after this synod but make no mistake about it, there's much work to do. We now need to distil all that happened over the three days – and that's a huge amount – into a practical plan. It needs to be well thought out and reflected on and there has to be a strategic review built into it. There also needs to be patience with the workload ahead. It will not happen overnight, but it will happen.

Finally, I feel incredibly affirmed as a priest by the whole process but particularly the synod itself. It has told me as a priest that I am not alone, that there are many, many people out there willing and wanting to share in the work of building up the community of faith, sharing in our baptismal calling to bring the good news of the gospel to the people of our diocese. This has been extremely reassuring for me and for all of us priests.

Chapter Eighteen
The Votes: Interpreting the Data
Rosemary O'Connor

Developing Action Proposals for the Synod
Once delegates had selected the six themes that formed the agenda for the synod, the process continued with a series of local workshops where delegates brainstormed a vision and potential actions to address the needs identified within each theme. Training and testing of an action proposal template was undertaken in readiness for the next round of workshops.

In the follow-up series of workshops, organised by theme, individual posters for the proposed actions were placed on the walls of the venues in line with the Open Space methodology.[1] Delegates were invited into a prayerful and reflective space. Inputs from the various synod gatherings of relevance to the theme were recollected (including talks given by Fr Paul Philibert, Sir Harry Burns and Dr Niamh Hourigan), along with readings from scripture. Delegates were invited to undertake a gallery walk of all the postered action ideas. Once they had

---

1. 'Open Space Facilitator Guide', http://www.algonquincollege.com/fol/files/2012/11/Open_Space_Facilitator_Guide_v1.doc

reviewed all the posters, they were invited to allocate red dot stickers to the ideas they felt were most critical to address the needs of the theme. The next step was for each delegate to go and stand by the poster (action idea) they were most drawn to. The group gathered around each poster (action idea) was then invited to draft a proposal using the action proposal template refined from the previous series of workshops.

The action proposals from each thematic workshop were presented to all delegates in a gathering on 12 March. This gathering was used as a dry run of the synod itself to test the format and procedures. Feedback from this gathering helped to refine and de-duplicate the action proposals. Following the 12 March gathering, a synod delegate workbook was prepared. This included 101 action proposals across the six synod themes.

Voting on Action Proposals during the Synod

During the synod itself, from 8 to 10 April, each of the themes were presented in the format of offering a vision for the theme, an input from Bishop Brendan Leahy and then action proposal by action proposal delegates were facilitated through a voting process using electronic voting 'clickers'. Delegates were given three voting choices as follows:

1. Yes, I strongly support this proposal and consider it a priority
2. Yes, I support this proposal
3. No, I do not support this proposal

During the synod, delegates were able to see in real time the distribution of votes across the three voting options for each action proposal. Figure 18.1 provides an example of the results that were presented immediately following a vote.

Following the synod, a working group tasked with interpreting the voting results was established and included

The Votes: Interpreting the Data

55%	30%	15%
Yes, I strongly support this proposal and consider it a priority	Yes, I support this proposal	No, I do not support this proposal

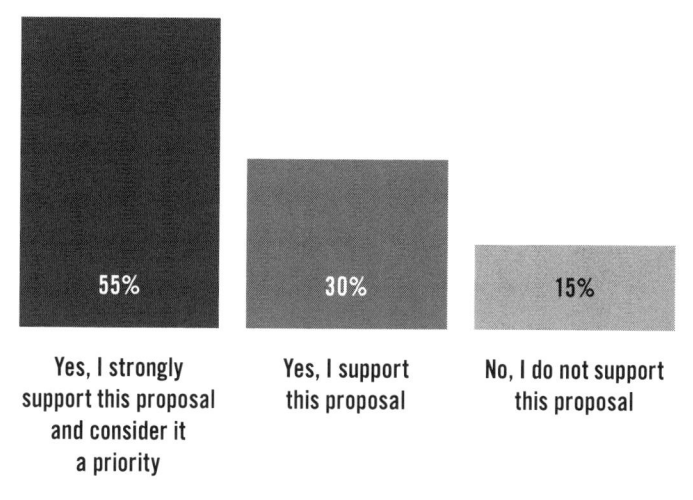

Figure 18.1: Example of Results Displayed during the Synod

Dr Éamonn Fitzgibbon (synod director), Dr Gerard Enright (mathematics), Dr Shane O'Sullivan (social research), Dr Jessie Rogers (scripture, research methodology) and Rosemary O'Connor (pastoral planning, research methodology).

Voting Levels throughout the Synod

The data provided through the electronic voting system was analysed in detail. The analysis revealed an interesting feature, which was not evident during the synod itself: the number of people voting changed throughout the voting process; i.e. there were varying levels of abstention. During a debrief session, held after the synod with the facilitators of small-group discussions during the synod as well as observers, a number of factors were identified that potentially contributed to the changing levels of voting. In some instances if people were unsure of what a proposal meant they abstained from voting, in other cases if someone voted in favour of a proposal and a second proposal came forward that duplicated or contradicted this they abstained. Some proposals were seen as having a specific geographic focus;

delegates who were from outside this geographic area did not vote as they didn't see its relevance to their jurisdiction. Figure 18.2 illustrates the voting levels throughout the synod.

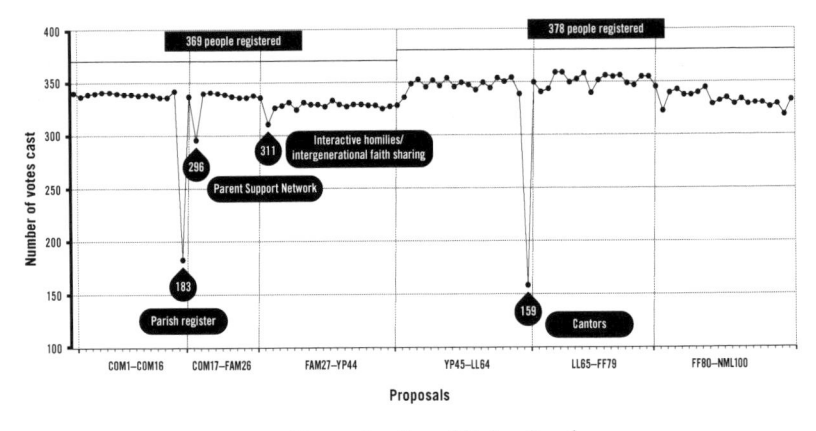

Figure 18.2: Synod Voting Levels

It was evident from the synod that people used their votes to give an indication of how they viewed the priority of any given proposal; only a very small number of proposals (three in total) received a majority of no votes. The working group arrived at the conclusion that the voting results needed to give an indication of priority; i.e. which proposals were considered the highest priority in each theme. It was clear that some form of weighting needed to be applied to the votes to arrive at a transparent and comparable scoring of proposals.

Applying Weighting Factors

From the data analysis it was evident that delegates exercised four options when considering each proposal: they voted 1 for proposals they considered a high priority; they voted 2 for proposals they were in favour of but didn't necessarily consider a priority; they abstained if they were unsure or didn't see the proposal as relevant to their own context; they voted 3 for

The Votes: Interpreting the Data

proposals they did not support. The working group considered various options for weighting the results. Ultimately, it was considered that the fairest weighting model was to assign a weighting of 2 to proposals delegates gave their number 1 'Yes, I strongly support this proposal and consider it a priority' vote to, proposals receiving a 'Yes, I support this proposal' vote (voting option 2) were given a weighting of 1, abstentions were given a zero weighting and proposals receiving a 'No, I do not support this proposal' vote (voting option 3) were given a weighting of -1. This weighting gave a clear picture of the delegates' collective view of the order of priority across all the themes. Figure 18.3 illustrates the weighting.

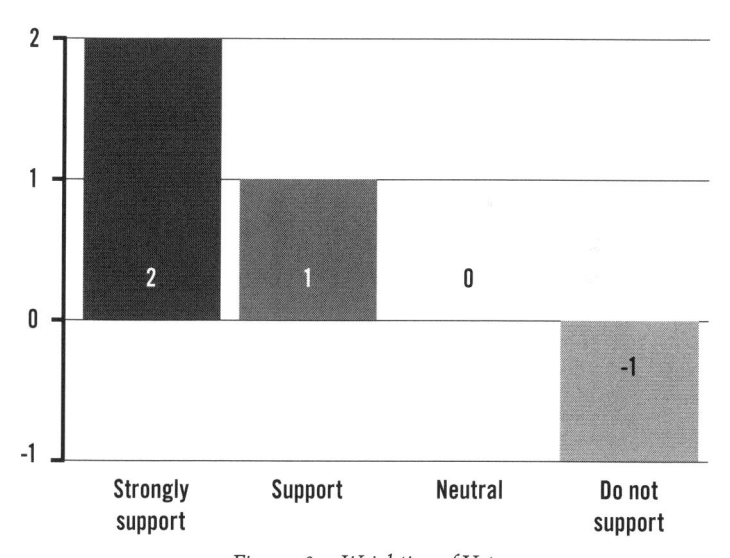

Figure 18.3: Weighting of Votes

The potential range of scores for any given proposal went from a theoretical maximum of 800 points based on a maximum of 400 delegates all giving a 'Yes, I strongly support this proposal and consider it a priority' number 1 vote (weighting of 2) to a proposal to a theoretical minimum of -400 points based on the maximum of 400 delegates all giving a proposal a number 3 'No, I do not support this proposal' vote (weighting of -1). In reality, nineteen of the 101 proposals scored 500 points or above and only ten proposals scored under 200 points.

Priority Ranking of Proposals

Once the weighting was applied, the voting data was analysed and a priority ranking was established for each theme. This ranking was used to guide the process of developing a diocesan pastoral plan by paying particular attention to the proposals given the highest priority as being the most urgent for the people of the diocese.

By way of example, Figure 18.4 illustrates the ranking of proposals for the Community and Sense of Belonging theme.

The Votes: Interpreting the Data

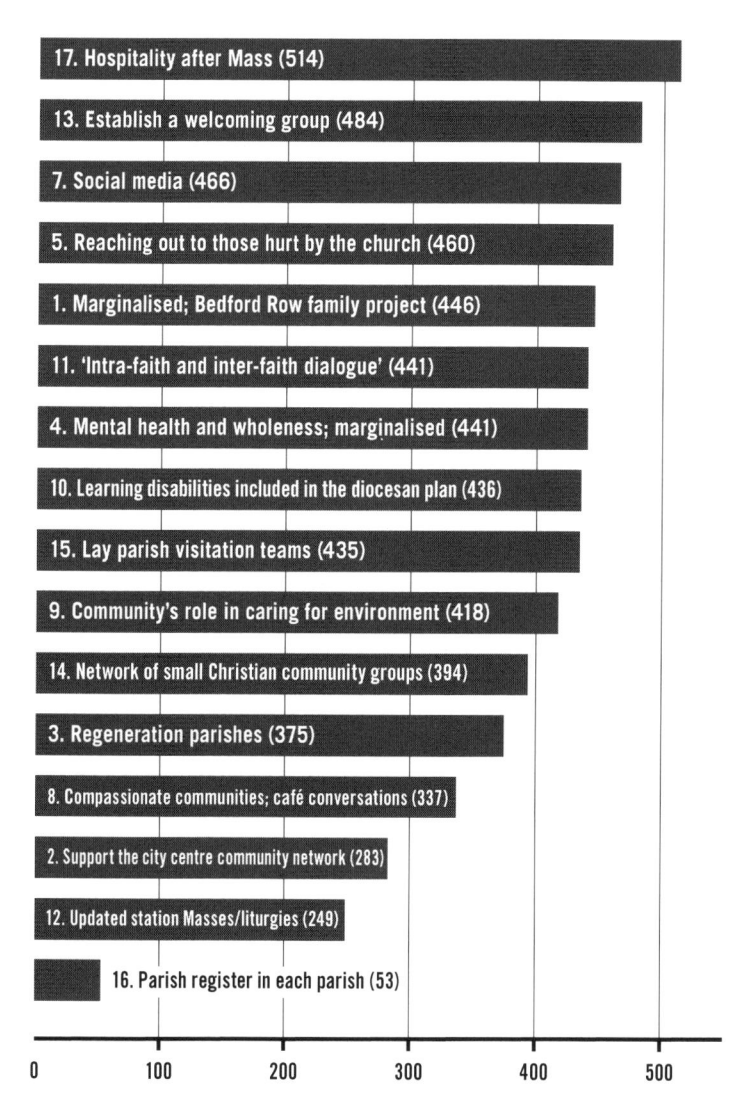

- 17. Hospitality after Mass (514)
- 13. Establish a welcoming group (484)
- 7. Social media (466)
- 5. Reaching out to those hurt by the church (460)
- 1. Marginalised; Bedford Row family project (446)
- 11. 'Intra-faith and inter-faith dialogue' (441)
- 4. Mental health and wholeness; marginalised (441)
- 10. Learning disabilities included in the diocesan plan (436)
- 15. Lay parish visitation teams (435)
- 9. Community's role in caring for environment (418)
- 14. Network of small Christian community groups (394)
- 3. Regeneration parishes (375)
- 8. Compassionate communities; café conversations (337)
- 2. Support the city centre community network (283)
- 12. Updated station Masses/liturgies (249)
- 16. Parish register in each parish (53)

Figure 18.4: Community and Sense of Belonging – Total Score

Chapter Nineteen
Post-Synod: Was it Worth it?
Bishop Brendan Leahy

I WOULD ANSWER QUESTIONS SUCH AS 'WAS IT WORTH it?' and 'Would we do it again?' with a very definite yes. Both the preparations and the event itself were rich experiences in many ways.

Participants engaged in a formative process that will remain regardless of particular outcomes. For many it was a profound immersion in the Church as a living organism rather than simply an organisation. At different times, there was a palpable sense of being in the presence of God, 'where two or three are gathered', savouring the divine at work. It also taught us the need to adapt attitudes of frankness and openness, to recognise fears and challenges, to be prepared to travel a journey.

I was particularly pleased that the dynamic of the proceedings was one of spiritual discernment. I believe we all grew in that art of discernment during the weeks and months of the synod journey. By linking scriptural inputs with a focus on mutual listening to and learning from one another, in a spirit of the New Commandment of love for one another, we became 'trained' in a way of communion that should always undergird decision-making in the Church.

Would we do things differently? Yes, of course. It was the first synod in a long time. It was a new experience for all of us. I suspect a future synod would not try to review the whole life of the Church. It would be sufficient to pick one or two topics or areas for review. It might be a shorter synod. We might devote greater time and attention to the catechetical dimension of the synod. It would be important to develop a regular frequent rhythm of synods.

What are the challenges as we move forward? The main challenge is to ensure the outcomes of the synod are 'implemented'. We now have a pastoral plan with many very fine proposals and tips for strategic planning and actions. But if they remain in a document then that would be a failure. Thankfully, as a diocese we have moved on some of the decisions taken at the synod.

Nevertheless, we must make sure it doesn't become an event of the past that we now move on from and forget! Worse still, no matter how much we tried to communicate about the synod, there will be some who weren't really part of it and now could figure the results of the synod are coming 'from above' whereas the whole synod event involved very much a bottom-up approach. It is strange to hear occasionally the accusation of 'top down' levelled at an event that involved five thousand people of the diocese. But it reminds me again and again of how we can never do enough to communicate so that all are participants in our diocesan life.

The biggest challenge now, it seems to me, is to keep the synod alive, not as an event to look back on, but rather as a style of Church. And that requires more than techniques, methods and programmes. It needs, above all, a new step in how we approach our spiritual life as members of the Church and not just as individuals.

What has characterised much of our spirituality is a conviction that we go to God by going within ourselves, discovering God ('his majesty', as Teresa of Ávila would say) within the 'inner chamber' of our soul. That is, of course, true. But there is a risk. Exterior engagement, relationships and Church activities can somehow be viewed as 'external' to our spiritual life. We try to animate our activities with what we have contemplated in our soul.

A synodal style of Church requires recognition that our spiritual life is also synodal. We journey with others to and in God. In the twenty-first century, we hear psychologists and philosophers, spiritual advisors and health specialists advise us on the importance of relationships. Christians increasingly recognise that we often didn't give sufficient attention to the fact that our relationships have been redeemed. God's grace is working not just *within* us but also *among* us. As St Pope John Paul II put it, we are called not just to contemplate the Trinity dwelling within us, but we are also created and redeemed to 'live the Trinity' in our relating to one another.

This explains why there is a greater focus on the core significance of Jesus' New Commandment, 'Love one another as I have loved you.' It is not merely a moral sentiment or a general ethical precept on the part of Jesus. It is his 'law' to govern our whole lives. Vatican II called it the 'law' of the Church.

The Spirit is helping us see that our way of interrelating, decision-making and organising need to be synodal in style. To adopt a synodal style is nothing less than to rediscover Jesus' teaching on love *for one another* as the key to the Church journeying together. In the power of the Spirit, we let him journey *among* us, guiding and enlightening us.

Conclusion

Éamonn Fitzgibbon

IN MANY WAYS THE PROPOSALS AT THE SYNOD ARE THE building blocks that enabled us to construct a pastoral plan for the future. However, before the blocks could be placed, we needed to construct a 'scaffold' that allowed us to create a plan. Essentially, this is a framework containing timelines and offers a menu of options for parishes, pastoral areas and the diocese to implement the decisions of the synod.

The creation of a broad strategic plan with key milestones gives a picture of where we are all going together – parishes, pastoral areas and diocese – but it doesn't imply that everybody has to be doing the same thing at the same time.

The task post-synod was to drill down into the results and interpret the findings, establish a set of diocesan statutes and a diocesan pastoral plan. These documents and a synod report were submitted to the Holy See and were subsequently promulgated in the diocese. Going forward, it will be important to be able to see and name the fruits of the Limerick Diocesan Synod 2016.

Postscript: What Does a Synodal Process Look Like?

Pope Francis' Letter on Synodality to the Church in Germany

Bishop Brendan Leahy

THE CATHOLIC CHURCH IN GERMANY IS WELL KNOWN for its generosity in helping the Church all over the world. It has also produced great saints and theologians. It has been to the fore in promoting ecumenism. But now the Church in Germany is facing new times and new questions, so the bishops there have proposed a synodal journey for the Church. Pope Francis has written a letter to accompany them. The letter is well worth reading in its entirety. This short chapter is a brief summary of the main points Pope Francis makes.

Two Main Themes and Two Approaches

There are two main themes running right through the letter. The first is that a synodal process will always need the guidance of the Holy Spirit. It can never be a case of people getting together and trying to work things out for themselves on the basis of their own ideas and insights, attempting to 'update' the Church but doing so without God. Synodality, Pope Francis writes, 'presupposes and requires the irruption of the Holy Spirit'. Otherwise, we risk a modern form of the ancient heresy of Pelagianism that proposed that salvation could be achieved by our own efforts without the assistance of God's grace.

A second theme is that a synodal journey involves the *whole* Church and is never just an exercise on the part of a single diocese or country on its own. We always need the humility to recognise that the Church has deep roots in God's plan as revealed in the gospel and is bigger than any of us and all of us. As Pope Francis puts it, we need to be 'living and feeling with the Church and in the Church and often this will bring us to suffer in the Church and with the Church'. The point for Pope Francis is that a synodal process should never see us boxed into our own particular angle or perspective as individuals or parishes or dioceses. Of course, we'll have our viewpoints, differences and debates but remember – we belong to a body bigger than us, the whole People of God.

When it comes to describing the process of discerning which directions the Church needs to take today, the Pope proposes a double perspective. On the one hand, there's what he calls 'synodality from below'. We might call this the grassroots level of the Church, involving lay people at all levels (parishes, councils, agencies). Pope Francis encourages special attention be given to those who might be considered the more simple and humble among us. We need to be attentive especially to the holiness found in families, workers, the sick and elderly religious.

But then there's also the 'synodality from above'. What Pope Francis has in mind here is that we don't build the Church by ourselves. The Church comes to us 'from above'; that is, through the scripture and tradition handed down to us throughout the centuries by the whole People of God, but in a particular way through the gift of the ministry of the bishops who are linked in communion with the Pope and with one another.

Pope Francis' Letter on Synodality to the Church in Germany

Updating the Church?

A synodal process is certainly about responding to the questions and issues facing the Church today. The Church is always in need of reform and 'updating'. But Pope Francis injects a note of realism when he reminds us that we shouldn't expect to be able to respond all at once to all the issues and problems. The Church will never be perfect in this world: 'The Church is and always will be a pilgrim in history, the bearer of a treasure in clay vessels' (cf. 2 Cor 4:7).

An attempt to 'update' the Church will always need what Pope Francis calls a 'long fermentation of life and cooperation by many over many years'. In other words, be careful not to be duped by immediate results that seem to generate quick hits in terms of media. A true synodal process will focus on building up the Church for what it is: the People of God, guided by the Spirit over time into the fullness of Truth. Some aspects of our community life will need to die, other aspects will need to be 'visited by the Lord' in a new way. But it shouldn't be viewed as trying to get the perfect system: 'You could have a well organised Church body, one that was "modernised" but without soul and Gospel newness' and the net result would be that 'we would be living in a "fizzy" Christianity, without Gospel flavour'.

The transformation required in a synodal process is not just change and updating but rather 'pastoral conversion': 'Seek first the Kingdom of God … and all the rest will be given to us' (Mt 6:33). Our way of seeing and doing things needs to undergo a deep conversion in love of God and of one another.

Evangelisation, Joy and Spiritual Medicines

The key to a synodal process for Pope Francis is evangelisation: 'Evangelisation must be our key criterion', meaning that we must start with evangelising ourselves before we want to go and propose change in and for others. And this should involve joy.

For Pope Francis, joy is the hallmark of whether we are on the right track or not. Yes, we will have moments of the Cross but deep down the peace our faith brings enables us to recognise the gifts of God in ourselves and in others. We always need to be wary of bad counsellors, such as bad humour and bitterness, defeatism and ingratitude.

A synodal process can't just be about analysis or discussions that go around in circles. Quoting his apostolic exhortation *Evangelii Gaudium* (74), the Pope speaks of a missionary enthusiasm. We need to reach out and 'anoint with the spirit of Christ all earthly realities in their many crossroads where new narratives and paradigms are being formed, bringing the word of Jesus to the inmost soul of our cities'. A synodal process should bring us to recognise Christ in the faces of suffering around us, in the individualism that is spreading and the new forms of slavery that entrap people today.

In discerning what the Spirit is saying today to the Church (Rv 2:7), a synodal process involves reading the signs of the times. But reading the signs of the times isn't the same as simply adapting ourselves to the spirit of the times. Pope Francis reminds us of something important that the Second Vatican Council rediscovered – the fact that all the baptised have been anointed and have what's called a 'sense of the Church'. And it is this sense of the Church that must be alive when making decisions at all levels.

Pope Francis refers to another ancient heresy – Gnosticism. A modern form of this heresy can be found in those who want to make a name for themselves with their own new ideas different from what the Word of God gives us. Accordingly, the Pope advises us to be wary of 'innovators' or 'enlightened ones' who claim to go beyond the 'we' of the Church. A synodal process needs to be alert to the fact that the 'Father of lies and division' can be at work and divide us as a people.

Pope Francis' Letter on Synodality to the Church in Germany

The Pope concludes his letter by recommending what he calls the spiritual medicines of prayer, penance and adoration. Ultimately, in a synodal process we need to be like Christ who 'emptied himself' in love of God and service of humanity (Phil 2:1–11). To speak, to act, to respond as the Body of Christ journeying together means to speak and act like Christ, with his very sentiments, ways and priorities. That's why the beatitudes indicate the way forward. They are like a mirror we can look into to see if we are on the right track.

Synodality in the Life and Mission of the Church

Extracts from a 2018 International Theological Commission Document

IN 2018 THE INTERNATIONAL THEOLOGICAL COMMISSION published a document entitled *Synodality in the Life and Mission of the Church*.[1] The first two chapters provide theological foundations for the image of the Church as synod, emphasising the Second Vatican Council's vision of the Church as the People of God participating in the life of the Trinity, living in missionary communion with one another and towards others. The third chapter looks at practical questions of how to make synodality 'happen' on local, regional and universal levels of the Church. It indicates the structures of participation that already exist. The fourth chapter explores the spiritual and pastoral conversion needed, underlining the communal discernment necessary for an authentic synodal experience of Church. The following is a selection of extracts from the fourth chapter of the document

---

1. International Theological Commission, 'Synodality in the Life and Mission of the Church', 2 March 2018, https://www.vatican.va/roman_curia/congregations/cfaith/cti_documents/rc_cti_20180302_sinodalita_en.html, accessed 2 July 2021.

that is well worth reading in its entirety. Footnote references have been omitted for ease of reading.

103. Synodality is established to energise the life and evangelising mission of the Church in union with and under the guidance of the Lord Jesus, who promised: 'where two or three meet in my name, I am there among them' (Mt 18:20); 'look. I am with you always; yes, to the end of the world' (Mt 28:20). The synodal renewal of the Church happens through the revitalisation of synodal structures, of course, but expresses itself first and foremost in response to God's gracious call to live as His People, who journey through history towards the fulfilment of the Kingdom.

104. 'Every renewal of the Church is essentially grounded in increase of fidelity to her own calling'. So, in carrying out her mission, the Church is called to constant conversion, which is a 'pastoral and missionary conversion', too; this involves renewing mentalities, attitudes, practices and structures, in order to be ever more faithful to her vocation. An ecclesial mentality shaped by synodal thinking joyfully welcomes and promotes the grace in virtue of which all the baptised are qualified and called to be missionary disciples. The great challenge for pastoral conversion that follows from this for the life of the Church is to intensify the mutual collaboration of all in evangelising witness based on everyone's gifts ...

107. (There is a) need for the Church to become 'the home and school of communion'. Without conversion of heart and mind and without disciplined training for welcoming and listening to one another the external instruments of communion would be of hardly any use; on the contrary, they could be transformed into mere heartless, faceless masks ...

Extracts from a 2018 International Theological Commission Document

109. The eucharistic *synaxis* (assembly) is the source and paradigm of the spirituality of communion. In it are expressed the specific elements of Christian life that are called to mould the *affectus synodalis* (a synodal attitude).

a. The invocation of the Trinity. The eucharistic *synaxis* (assembly) starts from the invocation of the Blessed Trinity. Gathered by the Father, in the outpouring of the Holy Spirit the Church becomes the living sacrament of Christ: 'Where two or three meet in my name, I am there among them' (Mt 18:19). The unity of the Blessed Trinity in the communion of the three divine Persons is revealed in the Christian community, which is called to live 'the unity of God's sons and daughters in truth and charity', in the exercise of the various gifts and charisms received from the Holy Spirit for the common good.

b. Reconciliation. The eucharistic *synaxis* (assembly) paves the way for communion by means of reconciliation with God and our brothers and sisters. The confession of sin celebrates the Father's merciful love and expresses the desire to follow not the way of division caused by sin but the path to unity: 'If you are bringing your offering to the altar and there remember that your brother has something against you … go and be reconciled with your brother first, and then come back and present your offering' (Mt 5, 23–24). Synodal events presume that we recognise our frailties and request forgiveness from each other. Reconciliation is the way to live the new evangelisation.

c. Listening to the Word of God. In the eucharistic synaxis (assembly) we listen to the Word in order to accept its message and let it illuminate our path. We learn how to hear God's voice by meditating on scripture, especially the Gospel, by celebrating the sacraments, above all the Eucharist, and by welcoming our brothers and sisters, especially the poor. Whoever exercises pastoral ministry and is called to break the bread of the Word along with the eucharistic bread needs to be familiar with the life of the community, in order to communicate God's message in the here and now of its life. The dialogical structure of the eucharistic liturgy is the paradigm of community discernment: before listening to each other, disciples must listen to the Word.

d. Communion. The Eucharist 'creates communion and fosters communion' with God and with our brothers and sisters. Generated by Christ through the Holy Spirit, communion is shared by men and women who, as baptised people, have equal dignity and receive different vocations from the Father and live them out responsibly – vocations which spring from baptism, confirmation, Holy Orders and from specific gifts of the Holy Spirit – to form a single body from many members. The rich and free convergence of this plurality in unity is what is set in motion in synodal events.

e. Mission. *Ite, missa est (Go, the Mass is ended)*. Communion made real in the Eucharist spurs us on to mission. Whoever partakes of the Body and Blood of Christ is called to share the joyous experience of it with everyone. Every synodal event prompts the Church to go outside the camp (cf. Heb 13:13) in order to bring Christ to people who are waiting to be saved by him. Saint Augustine says that we need 'to be of one heart and one mind on our journey *towards God*'. The unity of the community is not real without this inner *télos* (goal) which guides it along the paths of time towards its eschatological goal, 'that God may be all in all' (1 Cor 15:28). We must always face up to the question: how can we truly be a synodal Church unless we live 'moving outwards' towards everyone in order to go together towards God?

111. Synodal dialogue depends on courage both in speaking and in listening. It is not about engaging in a debate where one speaker tries to get the better of the others or counters their positions with brusque arguments, but about expressing whatever seems to have been suggested by the Holy Spirit as useful for communal discernment, at the same time being open to accepting whatever has been suggested by the same Spirit in other people's positions, 'for the general good' (1 Cor 12:7).

The criterion according to which 'unity prevails over conflict' is of particular value in conducting a dialogue, managing different opinions and experiences and learning 'a style of constructing history, a vital field where conflicts, tensions and opposites can reach a pluriform unity which generates new life', making it possible to 'build communion amid disagreement'. Actually, dialogue offers the opportunity to acquire new perspectives and points of view in order to shed light on the solution of the matter in question.

112. An essential attitude in synodal dialogue is humility, which inclines each one to be obedient to God's will and obedient to each other in Christ …

113. Exercising discernment is at the heart of synodal processes and events … Communal discernment allows us to discover God's call in a particular historical situation.

114. Communal discernment implies carefully and courageously listening to 'the groans' of the Spirit (cf. Rm 8:26) which emerge through the explicit or sometimes silent cry that goes up from the People of God: 'to listen to God, so that with Him we may hear the cry of His People; to listen to His People until we are in harmony with the will to which God calls us'. A disciple of Christ must be like a preacher, who 'has to contemplate the Word,

but he also has to contemplate his people'. Discernment must be carried out in a space of prayer, meditation, reflection and study, which we need to hear the voice of the Spirit; by means of sincere, serene and objective dialogue with our brothers and sisters; by paying attention to the real experiences and challenges of every community and every situation; in the exchange of gifts and in the convergence of all energies in view of building up the Body of Christ and proclaiming the Gospel; in the melting pot of feelings and thoughts that enable us to understand the Lord's will; by searching to be set free by the Gospel from any obstacle that might weaken our openness to the Spirit.

120. Pope Francis teaches that 'to walk together is *the constitutive way* of the Church; *the figure* that enables us to interpret reality with the eyes and heart of God; *the condition* for following the Lord Jesus and being servants of life in this wounded time'.

List of Contributors

Editors

Father Éamonn Fitzgibbon, DMin, a priest of the Diocese of Limerick, was the director of the Limerick Diocesan Synod. He is currently director of the Institute for Pastoral Studies, at the Department of Theology and Religious Studies in Mary Immaculate College, Limerick.

Karen Kiely was the administrator of the Limerick Diocesan Synod. Karen has worked in a variety of administrative positions with the Diocese of Limerick. She is married to Marc and is the proud mother of three children, Abbie, Seán and Ronan.

Contributors

Shane Ambrose works as a regional accountant at Concern Worldwide and has served overseas in the Republic of Sudan and Lebanon.

Sister Betty Baker, a Salesian sister, is a former principal of the Salesian Primary School and also worked as a pastoral co-ordinator with the Diocese of Limerick.

David Bracken works as the Limerick diocesan archivist.

LIST OF CONTRIBUTORS

Lorraine Buckley worked as a faith development coordinator in the Limerick Diocesan Pastoral Centre and is now Sr Marie Dominic OP, a member of the Dominican Sisters of St Joseph in the UK.

Canon Gerard Garrett is parish priest of Monaleen Parish.

Martin Kennedy works freelance as a trainer and facilitator with Church and community groups, and facilitated the Limerick Diocesan Synod.

Bishop Brendan Leahy has been bishop of Limerick since April 2013 and convoked the diocesan synod in September 2014.

Noirín Lynch worked as a pastoral coordinator in the Limerick Diocesan Pastoral Centre and is now director at FCJ Spirituality Centre, Spanish Point, Co. Clare.

Rosemary O'Connor is a director of Slí Nua Development, a training company, and is a theology graduate of All Hallows College who worked as a consultant to the synod process and is employed by the diocese as pastoral implementation manager.

Canon Tony Mullins is the parish priest of Abbeyfeale Parish and vicar-general of the Diocese of Limerick.

Sister Margaret O'Sullivan RSJ is the regional leader of the Sisters of Saint Joseph in Ireland, and has been engaged in parish ministry in the parish of Granagh-Ballingarry, Limerick.

Jessie Rogers is a lecturer in sacred scripture and is dean of the Faculty of Theology at the Pontifical University, St Patrick's College, Maynooth.